"I'm Frank Hamer"

"I'm Frank Hamer"

The Life of a Texas Peace Officer

H. Gordon Frost
and
John H. Jenkins

State House
Press
Buffalo Gap, Texas

Library of Congress Cataloging-in-Publication Data

Frost, H. Gordon
I'm Frank Hamer: The Life of a Texas Peace Officer
Gordon H. Frost & John H. Jenkins
  p. cm.
Includes Bibliographical references and index.
ISBN- 978-1-933337-64-7 (pbk. alk. paper)
ISBN- 933337-64-8 (pbk. alk. paper)
1. History United States 2. History / Texas History / Texas Rangers 3. United
  States: History-20th century. 4. Texas History / Texas Rangers Biography
  5. Barrow, Clyde 1904–1934 6. Parker, Bonnie 1910–1934
This paper meets the requirements of ANSI/NISO, Z39.48-1992 (permanence
  of paper) Binding materials have been chosen for durability ∞
I. Title.

"Cataloging-in-Publication Data available from the Library of Congress"

Manufactured in the United States
Copyright 2015, State House Press
Original Copyright 1968, Pemberton Press
All Rights Reserved

State House Press
P.O. Box 818
Buffalo Gap, Texas 79508
325-572-3974 • 325-572-3991 (fax)
www.tfhcc.com

Printed in the United States of America
Distributed by Texas A&M University Press Consortium
800-826-8911
www.tamupress.com

ISBN-13: 978-1-933337-64-7
ISBN-10: 1-933337-64-8

Book Design by Rosenbohm Graphic Design

CONTENTS

Photos to accompany Frank Hamer's story on pages 85 to 160.

INTRODUCTION

The transition in law enforcement that occurred between the times of the horseback frontier Ranger to the modern law officer of today was a long and difficult path. In perhaps no other officer was this transition more typified than in Captain Frank Hamer. Born in western Texas, reared as a cowboy and blacksmith, and trained in the aura of the Old West, Hamer joined the Texas Rangers when people still traveled by stagecoach and horseback. For the first half of his career as an officer, Hamer was in the saddle.

Then Texas entered modern times, and Hamer and law enforcement underwent a fundamental change. Automobiles replaced horses. Fingerprinting, ballistics, and new technological methods of criminology were introduced. Texas shifted gradually from rural to urban life, and the horseback Ranger became the highly knowledgeable specialist—part detective, part scientist, and thoroughly modern lawman.

In both eras Hamer possessed all the basic qualities of a great law officer. First, he was completely honest. His integrity was unimpeachable. Second, he was completely dedicated to his work. His work was his life; money, fame, and praise meant little to him. Third, he was absolutely fearless. He participated in probably more gunfights than any other Ranger of his times, was wounded seventeen times, left for dead four times, and never once backed away from a fight. Fourth, he was highly intelligent. His penetrating understanding of the criminal mind made him one of the best detectives Texas has even known. And, fifth, he never gave up. Whether he was tracking down desperadoes like Clyde Barrow and Bonnie Parker or solving a complicated murder case, Hamer never stopped until the case was solved.

Captain Hamer was famous as a law officer long before the Barrow–Parker case, but that chase is what climaxed his remarkable career. For 102 days he tracked the two murderers down, finally catching up with them for the first time on May 23, 1934, in Louisiana. And then, even though dealing with two of the most ruthless criminals in American history, he stood before them and offered to let them surrender before opening fire. His great ability and courage on that case brought acclaim throughout the nation—from the floor of Congress to the widows of the victims of Bonnie and Clyde's rampage.

Thousands of dollars were offered to Hamer for books, articles, and movies based on his life and career. Captain Hamer adamantly refused to accept any of the offers. He told his family to wait until after his death. Like many other honest officers, he had little to pass on to them except the rights to his story.

For three years now, John Jenkins and Gordon Frost have worked closely with the Hamer family to prepare this biography. It is a source of great satisfaction to us at the Texas Department of Public Safety that Captain Hamer's remarkable story is finally being told. The Texas Rangers are among Texas's most valuable and historic institutions, and Frank Hamer was one of the finest Rangers of them all.

Col. Homer Garrison
Director, Texas Department of Public Safety

His horse was the first to notice. The big sorrel gelding snorted nervously as the Comanche war party crept up on the sleeping trooper. Awaking with a start, Colonel Ranald S. Mackenzie's Fourth Cavalry regimental blacksmith realized instantly that he was surrounded by Indians—some of the most ferocious and hostile Indians in the entire West. Under such circumstances there is little a man can do. Little, that is, except what Trooper Frank Hamer proceeded to do.

Lurching drunkenly to his feet, he feigned insanity. Wheeling in and out among the brush, Hamer drooled at the mouth, alternately singing and mumbling gibberish. Proceeding directly toward the warriors he whistled, danced, and laughed. The Indians lowered their rifles in amazement. After the trooper had gyrated and whirled for a few more moments, one of the Comanches muttered in broken Spanish picked up from captured Mexicans: "Muy loco!"

In terror the Indians backed away from the crazed soldier. Fearful of the evil spirits that had taken possession of his body, they allowed him to pass, and without another word they mounted their horses and retired, thankful that they had not angered their gods by killing the possessed man.

As the last warrior passed out of sight, Trooper Hamer leapt on his horse and made tracks for Fort Clark.[1]

St. Louis-born and West Virginia-reared, Hamer had come to Texas in the late 1860s with Colonel Mackenzie, serving both as cavalryman and blacksmith for the U.S. Fourth Cavalry. As his escape from Comanches indicated, the tall, burly blacksmith had wits as well as brawn.

When his enlistment ended in 1874, Hamer married a pretty young Texas girl, Lou Emma Francis, and settled in the small community of Fairview, near present Floresville, Texas, where he opened a blacksmith shop. With the passage of time the couple had eight children, five boys and three girls: Estill, Sant, Francis Augustus, Harrison, Patricia, Alma, Flavius, and Grace.[2]

Some of the boys became farmers, some ranchers, some lawmen—and one became the greatest Texas Ranger of all time.

1

"I made up my mind to be as much like an Indian as I could."

Francis Augustus Hamer, the second-eldest child of Frank and Lou Emma, was born on St. Patrick's Day, March 17, 1884.[3] He was a large brown-haired, blue-eyed youngster, with a bright moon-shaped face. While he was still a child, the family moved to the Welch Ranch in San Saba County, and young Francis—or Frank or Pancho, as he was called—grew up around his father's blacksmith shop on the ranch.

Frank learned a lot on the Welch Ranch. Whenever he was not busy pumping the bellows or helping beat out horseshoes on the anvil, he learned to ride, rope, wrangle, and farm. Here also he received his only formal education, attending the local country school from the first through the sixth grades.

He enjoyed school, and sometimes, because of the distance between the ranch and the schoolhouse, he would stay overnight at school, sleeping on the benches until awakened in the morning by his teacher. He was a precocious student, especially in mathematics, and on many occasions the teacher would let him "hear a class" for her while she tended to other business. Often, the teacher would give the class some problem in arithmetic and Frank would have the answer almost immediately. The teacher would say, "Frank, why didn't you work out the problem? Where is your paper?"

To this Frank would reply, "I don't know how to work it on paper, Ma'am, but I can give you the right answer to the problem."[4]

Frank was not as much a reader as a mathematician. But he did read one 672-page book while still in school that had considerable influence on him: J. W. Wilbarger's *Indian Depredations in Texas*. The book is full of tales of the Texas Rangers and Indian fighters, and their battles and escapades with the Indians. J. Frank Dobie says of the book: "Texas was still country-living and frontier-minded in 1889, the year that J. W. Wilbarger's book was published." And it became "for generations household heritage among Texas families who fought for their land."[5] Surprisingly, the book did not give rise to a desire by Hamer to become a Texas Ranger. "I made up my mind," he explained later, "to be as much like an Indian as I could."[6]

The Hamer family moved to Oxford, Texas, in Llano County around 1894, and Frank's father established another blacksmith shop. The Llano area was good hunting country, and young Frank took to the woods whenever he could.

Taking only his old rifle, he would camp out and live off the land, not just overnight, but often for as long as two or three weeks at a time. He became a crack shot, for there was not enough money in the Hamer family for pleasure shooting. Muscles formed and hardened by the back-breaking work in the blacksmith shop became agile and wiry; and an inherited intellect, expanded in school and extended by the practical judgment and sound understanding of an experienced father, broadened as life in the woods added an Indian's cunning and an animal's senses.

Later during Hamer's life, an admirer wrote: "He slept on the ground and lived upon the game and fish which he took from the then unspoiled forests and streams of the beautiful hill country of Texas. On these excursions, he formed an intimate personal acquaintanceship with the insects, the birds, and the animals. The flight and signal call of birds, and especially the peculiar antics of the mockingbird, which takes a fighting attitude toward all the carnivora, told him where to look for predatory animals. He learned the habits of small animals, how to track them, and where to find their homes. He studied the bird-calls and the animal cries and practiced imitating them until he could call them to him. Almost anyone can call crows, but Frank Hamer can call quail, deer, road runners (paisanos), fox-squirrels, and hoot owls . . . . Hamer's sensory powers—sight, smell, hearing—may not be as acute as those of an Indian, but they are certainly far sharper than those of the average man. He doubtless inherited keen senses, but these he has cultivated and developed until his world of sense perceptions extends far beyond the horizon that bounds most mortals."[7]

At first his solitary jaunts, his schooling, and an occasional revival meeting led young Frank to desire to become a preacher. For nearly ten years during his childhood he believed he would take up the cloth when he grew up. By the age of sixteen, however, events began to occur which changed his plans. These events, mostly beyond his control, gave him the choice of two careers only: outlaw or lawman.

2

"I've come to settle accounts."

The days of hunting, fishing, and pleasant solitude ended for Hamer at the age of sixteen, when he and his younger brother Harrison, who was twelve, entered into a sharecropping agreement, "on the halves," with a man named Dan McSwain, who had several fields off Spring Creek in San Saba County. McSwain watched the industrious youngsters closely and was particularly pleased to notice what a fine shot Frank was—with rifle, shotgun, or pistol.

On an early day in June 1900, according to the story as told by Harrison, McSwain approached Frank and asked him how would he like to earn $150. Jokingly, Frank replied, "Who do I have to kill?"

McSwain's face grew serious as he mentioned the name of a prominent rancher with whom he was having some difficulties. Frank retorted, "Wait a minute now, Mr. McSwain, wait a minute! I was just kidding! I didn't mean that I was gonna kill anybody; that's the farthest thing from my mind. As a matter of fact, I want to be a preacher, and I just don't think that you can be a preacher and go about killing people."

McSwain said, "Well, if you're on that kind of bent, I'll up my offer to $200. I'll tell you what I want you to do: I'll hide you in a covered wagon and bring this man with me and we'll stand right in front of the wagon. While we're talkin', take out your pistol and shoot him through a slit in the canvas. Nobody will ever find out what happened, and you'll be $200 richer."

Harrison was standing behind a tree listening to this conversation. He heard Frank explode: "Hell no, I'm not gonna kill that man for you! As a matter of fact, I'm gonna tell him what you've proposed."

Frank turned on his heel. McSwain called after him, "If you let one word of this out, I'll kill you!"

That evening Frank and Harrison saddled their horses and rode to the intended victim's ranch and informed him of the plot to kill him. The rancher thanked the two boys for the information and told them he would be on his guard from then on.

Two days later, on June 12, 1900, Frank and Harrison were out plowing as usual. McSwain stopped them and told Harrison to go to the barn to get some equipment that they needed. He told Frank to get some groceries from the house. Harrison stopped to work on the plow, which was under a chinaberry tree, and Frank went into the house.

Harrison heard a noise behind him, turned around, and saw that Frank was squatting down picking up some cans he had dropped. Mc-Swain was creeping toward him with a shotgun. Harrison yelled to Frank, "Look out!"

When Harrison yelled, Frank looked up and jumped over to one side just as McSwain fired. The shot missed, but as Frank got up to run for cover, McSwain shot again. The powerful buckshot pellets hit Frank in his back and on the left side of his head, knocking him down. Frank drew a small pistol and fired back at McSwain. His first shot knocked McSwain down. His second clipped a limb off the chinaberry tree above Harrison. Rushing past the wounded McSwain, Harrison went to help his brother, who was struggling to his feet.

Harrison helped Frank up. The youths looked around and saw McSwain running to his house. They ran over a nearby hill and hid in a draw. McSwain came out with an old buffalo gun, mounted his horse, and began to search for the two frightened boys. He passed close by them, and Frank wanted to shoot him, but Harrison wisely whispered, "No, no, forget that. He's got that old rifle, and its bullet will reach a lot farther than your pistol, and carries a lot more weight."

The boys remained silent as McSwain went by. He rode across a creek and soon disappeared over a low rise, still looking for the boys. Harrison then helped his brother into their wagon, where Frank lay in agony from the multiple shotgun wounds. Harrison drove him back to Oxford where he was treated by a doctor.[1]

The wounds were slow to heal. Frank finally became so restless that he took his rifle and camping gear and left on his horse. He headed west until he hit the Pecos River and then followed it down 'til it met the Rio Grande, some fifteen miles east of Langtry, Texas, where the famous old Judge Roy Bean was holding his "court."

Healing in the warm rays of the West Texas sun, Frank explored the entire country. He discovered a large concave cliff with an Indian pictograph painted some fifteen to twenty feet up the side. It depicted a young Indian girl walking down a trail toward a water hole. Next to the trail was a large diamondback rattlesnake, waiting to strike. Frank also found a sealed cave, which he opened, and discovered a large room full of old Indian pottery.[2]

One of his favorite pastimes during this period of convalescence was sitting on top of a large mound of pebbles. In the evening he would sit on this mound and toss pebbles off the brink of a cliff into the water below. Day after day, having nothing to do, he pitched the small, round pebbles into the waters of the Pecos River. Eventually he threw enough of these pebbles until he had dug a hole in the mound waist-deep. He later told Marshall Kuykendall of Austin, "Marshall, it was some kind of grave. I stood up in this thing after I found out what it was and I found a shin bone that came up to my hip. You know, there was also a skull which was almost intact, and it was almost twice the size of a normal skull. I didn't know at the time that it was rare or valuable, so I just pitched it down, too."[3]

After his wounds had completely healed (although he carried some of the buckshot in his back for more than fifty years), Frank returned home to Oxford, deliberately passing through the McSwain Ranch on his way. There was still unfinished business to attend to. Riding up to the McSwain house, he called McSwain out.

"I thought I'd finished you!" McSwain exclaimed.

"Not by a damned sight," Frank replied. "I've come to settle accounts."

They drew their pistols and fired. McSwain's lifeless body slumped to the ground, and Hamer continued home to Oxford.[4]

At home he went at once to his mother and, according to the story told by the late Texas Ranger Chaplain, P. B. Hill, laid his hand on the family Bible and said, "Mother, I wanted to be a preacher, but from this hour on I'm making a vow to God I will pursue outlaws relentlessly and bring them to justice." This pledge, though it proved to be true, would be sorely tried during the next few years.[5]

3

"I'm Frank Hamer."

In 1901 Hamer and his younger brother Harrison left home for the last time. Their first job was wrangling for Barry Ketchum on his Pecos County ranch near Sheffield, Texas.[1]

Ketchum was a brother of the notorious outlaw, Tom "Black Jack" Ketchum. Black Jack and another brother, Sam, led a gang of outlaws that terrorized Arizona, New Mexico, and West Texas for nearly ten years. They robbed post offices, banks, and stores, held up stages, and robbed trains. In 1898 the gang split up and most of the others were killed or captured in a gunfight at Folsom, Arizona, on July 11, 1899.[2]

Black Jack, planning to retire from outlawry, decided to hold up one final train. He attacked the Colorado Southern, completely alone, and in a wild affray was wounded by the conductor and captured the next day. While the Hamer boys were working on Ketchum's ranch, Black Jack was hanged at Clayton on April 26, 1901. Frank never forgot the tales of the Ketchum gang and the bizarre hanging of Black Jack, during which his head was torn from his body.

By 1903 the two Hamers, still wrangling cattle, drifted down to Marathon to work on the McKenzie Ranch. While there, Frank and some of the other cowboys were sent to deliver a herd of horses to a buyer in San Angelo. Here Hamer's test of character occurred, and the pattern of his future life determined. Historian Walter Prescott Webb, in *The Texas Rangers*, describes what took place: "In his outfit was an experienced criminal who, because of his age and personality, had

9

considerable influence on the younger men. As the cowboys held the horses near town while the details of the trade were being completed, this outlaw suggested that it would be a simple operation to raid the bank and use the funds to establish a ranch in Old Mexico. Frank Hamer, among others, accepted the suggestion, and plans were hastily made. The men had moved to the head of the street that led by the bank and were about to make their play, when the foreman appeared and ordered them to take the horses to the delivery ground. This interruption no doubt saved the man who has left his mark on the tradition of law-enforcement in Texas. With a little time to think, Hamer realized what a fool he might have been and from that time forward he has done his own thinking. 'It was the adventure, and not the money, that appealed to me,' said the Captain. 'Had I gone into it, things would have been different.'"[3]

Once while working on the McKenzie spread, Hamer noticed three desert bighorn sheep in the distance. Out of curiosity he rode toward them. A fellow wrangler joined him and the two of them managed to cut one of the bighorns away from the others. The ram tried to cross the river and hesitated momentarily, being confused by the rapidly flowing water. Quickly Hamer shook out a loop, rode up to the ram, and roped him. The other wrangler came up and threw his loop around the hind legs of the ram. With the ram immobilized, Hamer got off his horse, took out his knife and cut the ram's throat. They threw his body onto the back of Hamer's saddle and took him to the chuckwagon where he was eaten by all of the cowhands, a welcome respite from their daily beef meals.[4]

During this same year, 1903, another incident happened to Hamer that forecast the future of the great Texas Ranger. Early one Saturday afternoon he rode into Winchell, Texas, to buy some sardines and crackers and to feed his horse. Naturally, he wore cowboy attire—boots, broad-brimmed hat, spurs—all of good quality, and unlike many cowpokes, clean and neat. The six-foot, two-inch, 193-pound youth noticed a boisterous Saturday-afternoon crowd hanging around the country store.

As Hamer approached the hitching post, one of the men in the group remarked: "Say, look there! That highpockets looks like he might give us a bit of fun!"

"My, my, ain't he pretty!" commented another.

Hamer ignored the crowd, dismounted, tied his horse, and went into the store. When he returned with his purchases, the roughnecks had made a circle around his horse. Frank, unruffled, put his purchases into his saddlebags and put the morral, or feed bag, on the horse's head. The toughs began to talk about how they would divide his clothes, one claiming his hat, another his boots, while others debated what form of punishment to put to Hamer himself.

"Why, he ain't even wet behind the ears," one drawled. "Someone get the tar," heckled another.

Hamer, not yet twenty years old, leaned nonchalantly against the hitching rail and began to whittle on a match.

The ringleader swaggered toward him, and one of the group warned, "Don't tear his britches; they'll fit me just fine!"

The bully came face to face with Hamer. "Who are you, sonny?" he demanded with a leer.

Hamer was ready. He looked up steadily for a long moment, then spat squarely into the big man's face.

In amazement the bully glowered at him, who continued to whittle on the match with his razor-sharp knife.

For an eternity the bully stared, sizing up his adversary, then intelligently turned and walked away. The youthful cowboy mounted his horse to depart, looked briefly at the stunned crowd, and answered calmly: "I'm Frank Hamer."[5]

4

"I wouldn't have sold out very cheap that day."

Sitting on the front porch of the Hamer home during the 1930s, historian Webb and Hamer would chat about Hamer's early life as a cowboy. Webb wrote:

"Frank Hamer began to ride early and continued in the saddle until paved highways and automobiles made the horse impractical in the pursuit of criminals. But his love of horses is still deep, as one can see when he talks of Bugler, a powerful bay animal that was his favorite and real companion. He handled his horses gently, but with the hand of a master, and can make you believe that a horse and man can come to understand each other perfectly if associated on long journeys, provided both have horse sense. He believes that the endurance of a horse on long or hard journeys depends more on the rider's knowledge of how to ride than on his weight. Though Hamer weighed nearly two hundred pounds, he could help the horse in such a way that he could hold with those of lesser burden. One must sit deep in the saddle, bear a part of his weight in the stirrups, and catch the rhythm of the animal. If the ride is long, there must be no galloping, but only the trot and walk. The cinch must be neither too loose nor too tight. Long hills must be taken at a walk, and, if time permits, with loose cinch for easy breathing."[1]

Hamer's love of horses was that of any good cowboy, and his hatred of horse thieves was just as deep.

He went to work in 1905 on the Carr Ranch, located between Sheffield and Ft. Stockton. While he was working there, horse thieves stole two good cowhorses, along with their saddles and bridles. The young wrangler was incensed and took out alone after the thieves.

Several days later he came up on the two men with their stolen mounts. Dismounting, Hamer ducked ino a small gully, circled, and took the two men by surprise. Winchester in hand, he led the two to the Crockett sheriff and returned the horses and equipment to a grateful boss.[2]

In October of that year Hamer was alone at the Carr headquarters, overseeing while his boss was away on business. Not having much to do one night, Hamer, like so many thousands of others across the country about that time, listened in on the brand new telephone party line that had recently been installed. He and the other ranchers would chat, comment on how well they could hear each other, and talk interminably about the weather.

One particular night Hamer listened as Sheriff D. S. "Dud" Barker talked to a former deputy sheriff, Charlie Witcher. A horse had been stolen from a Mr. Joy, and Sheriff Barker tried to get his former deputy to apprehend the thief, who had headed toward Witcher's ranch. The Carr Ranch lay in between.

"I'm sorry, Dud," replied Witcher, "I got my own things to take care of. Why don't you go after him yourself?"

"I can't," replied the sheriff, "I'm so busy here at the jail in Ft. Stockton that I hardly have time to leave and get my meals. Besides, that coyote has had such a jump, it would take me quite some time to catch up with him."

"'I'll go get him sheriff!" a voice broke in. Barker asked, "Who the hell are you?"

"I'm Frank Hamer, and I work out here on the Carr Ranch."

"He's headed your way," said the sheriff, "and if you can catch him I'll be mighty happy. I'll tell you what he looks like."

"You don't have to," Hamer said. "I just heard you describe him to Witcher."

"I'd be much obliged if you do catch him," said the sheriff. "I'll ride out there tomorrow to give you a hand."

Being familiar with the surrounding country, Hamer reckoned that the horse would not be able to reach the Carr Ranch until early the next morning. Because the only water for miles was at the Carr's windmill, he figured that would be where the criminal would stop. Hamer got up early and rode to the windmill, waiting nearby with his Winchester.

At daybreak he saw a mounted figure riding down a slope toward the windmill. Hamer waited until the horse thief dismounted and began to water his horse. Leveling his carbine on the man, Hamer stepped out from the brush.

"I'm Frank Hamer," he stated. "You're under arrest."

Seeing that he was covered, the man raised his hands in surrender. Hamer walked over and relieved him of his forty-five.

It was a significant experience for the young man. "Believe me," he later said, "I sure felt good that morning, going up and down the long slopes with that thief ahead of me. Finally, after riding sixteen miles, I saw Dud Barker top out on a hill two miles off. He was driving a couple of fast horses to a light buggy and they were sure stepping. I wouldn't have sold out very cheap that day."[3]

He greeted the sheriff and handed over the horse thief. Sheriff Barker handcuffed the prisoner, and remarked to Hamer, "This is the second time you've done my work. You did a mighty fine job of catchin' this man, Frank. How'd you like to be a Texas Ranger?"

"I never gave it too much thought before," replied Hamer. "It sounds pretty good, though. What do I have to do to get in?"

"You let me take care of that," answered the sheriff.

5

"When I see him comin' I jes' steps aside."

On February 23, 1906, Sheriff Barker wrote to the Adjutant General in Austin recommending Hamer as a Ranger. He mentioned Hamer's work in capturing the horse thief and remarked that he "has the ability to grasp the situation quickly."[1]

The adjutant was impressed. After some further inquiries, Hamer was approved. John H. Rogers, an old-time Ranger captain, wrote Barker to have Frank report to Sgt. Jim Moore, Company C, Texas Rangers at Sheffield. On April 21, 1906, Frank A. Hamer enlisted as a private in the Texas Rangers. He was twenty-two years old, six feet three inches tall, and weighed 193 pounds.[2]

Excitement came quickly. The situation with Mexican bandits along the border increased to the extent that Governor S. W. T. Lanham was forced to send Rogers' Ranger company to aid the U.S. Army posts along the Rio Grande. So high was the respect for the Texas Rangers that the company of seventeen men was considered sufficient reinforcement for the hundreds of federal troops who had been unable to maintain order. Hamer's company arrived at Del Rio on September 29, 1906.

In addition to border troubles, the Rangers were faced with keeping law and order in the Del Rio area. Del Rio was a no-man's-land to which crooks and riffraff from both Mexico and the United States flocked whenever things got too hot elsewhere.

One such desperado was Ed Putnam, alias Ed Sibley. This cruel, cold-blooded killer came to Del Rio a few weeks after Hamer's company arrived. He stayed at the local hotel-saloon and posed as a livestock dealer. In November he murdered a sheepman named J. W. Rolston near Box Springs and took his victim's large herd of sheep to a spot near Del Rio. He approached a local sheep rancher, B. M. Cauthorn, with the proposition that the two go in together to purchase "some sheep he knew of" at a bargain price. The idea appealed to Cauthorn, so Putnam took him to inspect Rolston's sheep. After seeing them, Cauthorn agreed to put up his half of the purchase price, which amounted to several thousand dollars. Several days later, on December 1, 1906, Cauthorn rode out of Del Rio with Putnam, carrying his share of the money with him. When they had ridden a few miles, Putnam drew his pistol and shot Cauthorn in the back.[3]

Taking Cauthorn's cash, he started toward the sheep herd, apparently intending to repeat the same performance at another town. But there had been a witness to the murder, and Putnam noticed him coming at a gallop with pistol drawn. Abandoning the sheep, Putnam raced away. After a short chase, Putnam holed up in the house of Glass Sharp, just north of the Del Rio railroad tracks. The witness wisely came no farther and returned to town to inform Captain Rogers of what had transpired.

Taking Hamer, R. M. "Duke" Hudson, and two other Rangers, Captain Rogers rode out to the Sharp place. Reining to a halt in the front of the house, Rogers called for Georgia Sharp, Glass Sharp's oldest daughter, to come out and talk. He told Georgia that he knew Putnam was in the house, informed her of what Putnam had done, and advised her to get the rest of the family out of the house, as there might be gunfire. Georgia went into the house and, moments later, Glass Sharp, his wife, and the rest of their children hurriedly left the house. Georgia stayed behind, trying to talk Putnam into giving himself up, to no avail. She ran out of the door holding her hands over her ears, expecting the gunfight to begin at any moment.[4]

"He won't come out, Captain Rogers," the hysterical girl cried. "He's got a funny look in his eyes and says he won't give up!" At that moment a shot rang out from the house.

The five Rangers dispersed, sought cover in various places surrounding the house, and opened fire. Miraculously, in the ensuing hour-long fight the outlaw was not fatally wounded by any of the Rangers' bullets. Running from window to window with the desperation of a cornered wild animal, Putnam fired at the Rangers whenever the opportunity presented itself.

Hamer moved from one position of cover to another, seeking a better spot from which to shoot. A movement in the house caught his attention. He paused behind a hackberry tree and watched as Putnam pulled a curtain back with his gun barrel and fired. The curtain quickly closed. Again, the curtain was pulled aside as the outlaw shot once more. The third time, Hamer was ready. As the curtain was being pulled aside, Hamer carefully aimed his Winchester carbine and squeezed off a shot. The bullet struck the crouching Putnam below the left cheekbone, traveled through his left jaw, and reentered the top of his left shoulder, finding its resting place in his heart. The outlaw slumped forward across the windowsill, his pistol thudding to the ground.

Captain Rogers called for his men to cease firing. Entering the house, the Rangers found the furniture in ruins. They counted more than three hundred bullet holes in the walls, and noted that even the cast iron legs of the cook stove had been cut off. Putnam's pockets contained many more shells, and had not Hamer's bullet been true, he would have been able to hold them off until dark, and been able to escape. Why Putnam passed up the chance to use Georgia Sharp as a hostage to escape is not known.[5]

The Del Rio paper reported: "Never before in the history of Del Rio were the citizens worked up to such a degree of sorrow and excitement as they have been since last Friday evening"; and young Frank Hamer tasted the sweet reward of a city's appreciation.[6]

Hamer continued as a Texas Ranger throughout 1907 and 1908. He and another Ranger took three-month shifts with two other Rangers as guards over a mining operation at Terlingua, spending the off-months scouting Southwest Texas for lawbreakers and Mexican *bandidos.*

In the fall of 1908 Hamer was approached by the city council of Navasota, Texas, to become City Marshal. The lawless element of the town was among the worst anywhere, and there was an atmosphere among many of the old-time families of handling the law without judge or jury. More of a Southern town than a Western one, Navasota's three thousand citizens included a large percentage of sharecroppers and negroes who were constantly at odds with illiterate bullies from the old families who openly flaunted the law. The Navasota newspaper, whose editor "went fishing" whenever a controversy arose, had recorded literally dozens of shoot-outs in the country during 1906, 1907, and 1908, and at least a hundred citizens had met violent deaths.

John Dibbrell suggested to the council that Hamer be hired. The previous marshal had lasted exactly one week, and someone had to be found who would take the job. Despite his youth, Hamer was pressed to accept. The bad element thought it could bully the youngster and so a majority of council votes was easily obtained.

Hamer loved nothing better than a challenge and accepted readily. On December 3, 1908, the Navasota *Examiner-Review* reported: "Mr. F. A. Hamer arrived yesterday and at once qualified as police officer of the city . . . made vacant by the resignation of W. B. Loftin."[7]

Hamer faced his first crisis on that very day. The patriarch of one of the old families decided to teach the new marshal a lesson. Trailed by a crowd of people the bewhiskered old man walked along the board sidewalk beside the muddy rain-soaked main street until he was just opposite the marshal's office. At that point he threw his head back and let forth with an ear-piercing rebel yell. Hamer stuck his head out the door to see what had happened. The man continued to yell at the top of his voice.

Marshal Hamer stepped solemnly across the loose boards that made a path to the other side of the street. "I'm Frank Hamer, the new City Marshal," he said calmly. "You know there's an ordinance against disturbing the peace. If you yell again I'm going to put you in jail."

The old man looked him in the eye, then let out another loud yell.

Hamer told his son many years later: "I knew that it was going to be decided right then and there whether or not I would continue as Marshal of Navasota."

"I just reached up with my left hand and grabbed a handful of White beard, put one foot up on the sidewalk, stepped back, and threw him like you would throw a cow. I put him right out in the middle of that mud. Then I turned to the crowd and said, 'Now, I told him what was going to happen: he's going to jail."

Hamer marched the old man quickly off to the town's small jail and charged him with disturbing the peace. The young marshal had won round one.[8]

Round two came a week later, when a citizen dropped by the marshal's office and began to chat with Hamer. He told Hamer about certain of the leading citizens, probably Ku Kluxers, who took care of certain aspects of law enforcement. "We don't allow our kind," he said, including himself in the group, "to be arrested." He told Hamer this meant even when they had had too much to drink and raised hell in town. The marshal was instructed to confine his duties to the negroes and "outsiders."

That night one of these upright, influential citizens got roaring drunk and started shooting up one of Navasota's saloons. Pushing through the batwing doors, Hamer told the offender he was under arrest. Looking around slowly, Hamer challenged the hostile faces that met him: "I understand you don't allow 'your kind' to be arrested."

He paused, hands on his hips, a slight smile playing on his lips. The crowd did not move. Marshal Hamer then escorted the drunk to jail.[9]

Word spread that Navasota had a City Marshal who was not afraid to perform his duty, and many of the town's wide-open dice and poker games quietly closed down. The horse races and cock fights moved away. Quietly and thoroughly, Frank cleaned up the town.

Such a task naturally brought him many enemies, who never ceased to give the young marshal a hard time. The proprietor of the main hotel, for example, had a pet bulldog that was feared with much justification by most people who saw him. The dog killed many other pets and bit a number of passersby, until finally the city council passed an ordinance requiring the man to confine or muzzle his bulldog. Shortly thereafter, Hamer rounded a corner and found the bulldog engaged in a fight with a fine bird dog, which had been leashed to a wagon by the farmer who owned it. By the time Hamer reached the dogs, the bulldog had a death grip on the other dog's throat. Hamer quickly slapped the bulldog with the barrel of his pistol. The hotel owner ran up and complained loudly that Hamer had mistreated his "pet."

"I had to," replied Marshal Hamer, "'cause your dog was just seconds away from killing that bird dog. As a matter of fact, your dog has disposed of quite a few pets around here as well as hurting a number of people. Now, if you want a watchdog, that's fine, but keep him on your premises or put a muzzle on him."

The hotel man sneered. "What'll you do if I don't?"

"If he ever attacks another animal or person without cause, I'll have to kill him," replied the marshal.

The hotel owner just laughed and walked away.

Several days later the dog, still running loose, killed a bird dog belonging to Herbert Terrell. Terrell complained to Hamer, and Hamer went immediately to the hotel lobby, where he drew his pistol, and killed the bulldog.

Holstering his pistol, Hamer told the shocked audience: "Maybe now you'll believe that when I say I'm going to uphold the law, I mean what I say."[10]

The good citizens, of course, rallied to Hamer's side in all these minor disputes. The problem was that so many of the men in positions of influence were not good citizens. The newspaper editor was a fence-rider. He never printed anything directly against Hamer, but he was also one of the night-riding group and wrote heated editorials calling for the negroes to be run out of town. His reports of the marshal's activities were full of innuendoes.

When Hamer left for a week's vacation that summer, an attempt was made to murder his deputy marshal, a man named Averetts. The newspaper reported: "Mr. Averetts has no enemies in Navasota . . . . The only theory which would seem to hold water is that someone who had it in for Hamer must have figured that the assassination of Mr. Averetts might have a depressing effect upon Hamer, probably causing his resignation to be handed in. This idea seems to prevail and has been advanced several times since the shooting by a number of citizens."[11]

The marshal took it all in stride, becoming perhaps just a little bit tougher, if such were possible. Webb describes it this way: "The town split into Hamer and anti-Hamer factions with the hotel man leading the anti-Hamer group which was recruited from saloon toughs, some of whom had felt the heel of the Hamer boots—and some the toe. The young marshal's struggle for supremacy was desperate, and in the course of time more of the toughs made contact with his boots. The situation was one that would permit no compromise, one in which the officer could show no weakness without complete loss of prestige. The details of the struggle cannot be given, but if related, would read like a chapter from the life of Wyatt Earp. This does not mean that anyone was killed, but some pretty well marked for future identification."[12]

Hamer got quite a reputation for the use of his feet in subduing criminals. "My feet were always loaded," he once remarked.[13] Often, when surrounded by a crowd of toughs, he would simply lash out with his feet, kicking them in the shins or the groin or anyplace that might be handy, with this surprise tactic winning the day. Hamer's one-time boss, Texas Adjutant General W. W. Sterling, likened Hamer's effective foot work to *savate*, the French science of foot fighting. According to General Sterling, "from the way he performed, I thought perhaps some adventure-seeking Frenchman had drifted into the Pecos country and showed him how it was done in France. His answer was that he had never taken any lessons other than those given by experience. In youthful fights when older boys ganged up on him, he discovered that his feet could be turned into high powered weapons, Hamer continued to use them in later battles."[14]

Hamer seldom used his fists in a fight. He would almost invariably slap his opponent with his open hand. His blacksmith arms were so powerful that a man so slapped would generally tumble to the ground as if poleaxed. General Sterling wrote: "When he boxed along side the head, it reminded me of a grizzly bear cuffing a steer."[15] All else failing, Hamer would use his pistol.

By the end of 1910, Hamer had singlehandedly made Navasota a safe place to live. Even the newspaper editor began to change his attitude. An instance of this change occurred when Bryan officers called Hamer to be on the lookout for a stolen horse and buggy. Seeing a buggy fitting the description given, Hamer and his deputy pursued the man on a wild chase for thirteen miles. The newspaper reported: "One of the men had gotten out of the buggy to open a gate when the officers arrived. They told him that they would arrest them for stealing the horse and buggy and the man opening the gate attempted to get back into the buggy when the officers made him throw up his hands. The man in the buggy refused to be arrested and drew his pistol. Then the officers fired and killed him, then took the other prisoner and carried him back to Navasota," where he was kept for the Brazos County sheriff.[16] This article, still not complimentary, at least contained no muffled criticisms as before.

When the Throop Saloon was burglarized, the editor wrote: "Marshal F. A. Hamer was notified and this indefatigable officer spent all night on the case and worked so successfully that Mr. Meyers was in possession of the whole amount stolen by ten o'clock the next morning."[17]

On the first of April 1911, Hamer was on the train, going north from Hempstead to Fort Worth. As the Navasota *Examiner-Review* later reported:

"Last night as the northbound passenger train on the Central was humming along at a pretty fair rate of speed about one and one-half miles north of Courtney, the engineer noticed an obstruction on the track and reversed his engine as quickly as possible, though it was not in time to prevent hitting it slightly. Two heavy railroad ties had been securely wedged between the rails with a lot of rock and had the engineer not seen the pile when he did the result would have been something awful to contemplate."

"Marshal F. A. Hamer of Navasota happened to be on the train and the engineer and fireman told him of seeing two negroes on the track a short distance back, walking toward Courtney. Mr. Hamer immediately hurried down the track toward Courtney afoot where, after a few moments of pretty slick work he found them in the act of going to bed. He asked if they were not the negroes in a disturbance on the northbound passenger out of Hempstead and negro like, they took the bait completely under, stating that they had not been on the train at all but had just come into town, walking from Navasota. Mr. Hamer promptly arrested both of them and started to Navasota with them afoot, but on reaching the tank four miles south of town the southbound passenger came along and he flagged it, taking the negroes on to Hempstead, returning this morning on the cutoff."

"Mr. Hamer visited the scene this morning and discovered evidence which he thinks sufficient to hang both the desperadoes."

"This is one of the prettiest pieces of detective work pulled off in his part of the country for months and adds another feather to Mr. Hamer's cap. He certainly does deserve unstinted credit for the smooth manner in which he trailed the negroes and caught them and while he is too modest, perhaps, to say anything about it, the railroad company is certainly under obligations, for there is no question but what the attempt would have been repeated at the earliest possible moment and maybe with disastrous results to both passengers and the railroad."[18]

One night, Foreman E. N. Simmons of the railroad ran to Hamer's office and reported that he had been robbed by a large negro. Hamer began a search, and at the railroad yards came upon a man who had an air of guilt about him that Hamer seemed almost able to smell. After a few casual questions, Hamer asked where he had come from. The man replied that he had just come from Hempstead. Hamer looked at him with an exaggerated suspicion, and said, "Hempstead, eh?"

The man, thinking he had been caught in his lie, said: "No, I means Waller."

By now, Hamer knew he had the guilty party. He really had no reason to believe the man had not come from Hempstead, but by his feigned suspicion had put the man into a sweat—the mark of a person with something to hide. Hamer searched him and found Mrs. Simmons' wedding ring and other valuables.

At this point the man broke away and ran. Hamer shouted to him to stop, then fired twice into the air. He still ran, so Hamer "then sent two shots to kill." The *Examiner-Review* reported: "The negro, Manny Jackson, alias Kid Jackson, shot by Special Officer Hamer at the depot Tuesday night about 12 o'clock, died late yesterday afternoon."[19] The man had been a much wanted criminal who had escaped from prison and was wanted by the law in several states.

The negro's general attitude toward Hamer was best expressed some years later by a porter in an Austin barbershop. A customer brought in some pictures of the Texas Rangers, and one of the barbers held up Hamer's picture for the porter to see.

"Do you know him?" the barber asked.

"Yes suh," said the porter with a wide grin, "an' when I sees him comin' I jes' steps aside."[20]

In 1918, seven years after leaving Navasota, Hamer and his bride were passing through Reno in a new touring car. Suddenly a large negro jumped from the sidewalk right into the street and, smiling broadly, shouted, "Hello, Cap!"

Hamer smiled and waved, telling his wife: "That's a negro from Navasota. When I was marshal down there, the Brazos bottom had a lot of plantations with many field hands, who picked cotton and raised other field crops. I found that this fellow was the unofficial boss of all the rest down there, and anytime they had a parade or anything, such as a Juneteenth celebration, I'd go over to this man, and say: 'Now, Sam, I'm gonna make you the parade marshal. I want you to keep all the rest of the boys in line, so pick out three or four helpers and make sure everyone behaves. I'd given Sam a great big, wide red sash and he'd put this around his shoulders and wear a tall black silk tophat. All of the time that I was there, we never had any trouble at a negro celebration, thanks to Sam."[21]

On April 20, 1911, Hamer resigned as City Marshal of Navasota to go to Houston to work as a special officer for Mayor Baldwin Rice. Commenting on his resignation, the Navasota newspaper editorialized: "Hamer has tendered his resignation to the City Council, effective as soon as a satisfactory officer has been secured to take his place. Mr. Hamer has been besieged with offers from Mayor Rice of Houston for several months, all of which have been refused on account of the fact that an available substitute for his position was not to be had. Mr. Hamer has made a most efficient officer since coming to Navasota, and is universally liked. He plays no favorites in the discharge of his duty—everybody looks alike to him, and if an offender of the law labors under the impression that he can raise a disturbance and get off with it all he has to do is to try him on. Of course such a man has his enemies; it is natural to suppose that he wouldn't have, but as an impartial peace officer he holds the championship so far as we are informed. He leaves Navasota with the best wishes of the City Council, with whom he has always been in harmony and the further knowledge of having made many warm personal friends."[22]

6

"He has the reputation of being quiet, steady, and a gentleman."

Special Officer Hamer went to work for Mayor Rice in Houston on April 21, 1911. His first assignment was to assist other special officers in tracking down a gang that had been responsible for killing several Houston policemen. After this, Hamer, along with Harris County Sheriff M. Frank Hammond, captured the notorious Matthew Young, alias "Mississippi Red."

On June 14, 1911, a warrant was issued for the arrest of Mississippi Red, charging him with wife-beating. Constable Isham Isgit went to Red's house in Harrisburg, now part of Houston. Knocking on the door, the constable identified himself and called for Mississippi Red to surrender. No sooner had these words been spoken than the large negro shot and killed Constable Isgit. Red then fled to Louisiana.

Sheriff Hammond was not sworn in until a few months later, and Mississippi Red was still at large. The day after he became sheriff, Hammond asked Mayor Rice to assign Hamer to the Mississippi Red case, as the Houston homicide squad had failed to capture him. Mayor Rice consented, and Hamer determinedly set out to apprehend the murderer. While Sheriff Hammond attended the routine affairs of taking over the sheriff's department, Hamer quietly gathered information on the fugitive. He learned that Red had gone first to the town of Red Cross, Louisiana, where he worked on the Melville Levee, next to the Atchafalaya River, repairing the levee that had been severely damaged by a flood. Working with nearly 5,000 others in the bottoms of the Mississippi delta, Young was practically buried from the rest of the world.

Young had an insatiable penchant for crap shooting. Each payday he would slip out of the work camp to Opelousas or some other town to gamble. At this time he adopted another alias, and he was known around that neighborhood as "Poor Boy" Taylor and had a reputation for being mean and bad. Hamer took this information to Sheriff Hammond, and the lawmen obtained the necessary extradition papers for the fugitive's arrest.

Sheriff Hammond and Hamer left Houston on the afternoon of December 24 and proceeded to Opelousas, to pick up the trail that Hamer had uncovered. By this time they found that Young was somewhere near Baton Rouge and learned that he had been seen at Melville. At Melville, he was traced to the levee.

Sheriff Hammond later said: "It is so easy to evade capture in the woods and brakes throughout that region that we succeeded in our efforts only through strategy and utmost care and precaution. On arriving at Red Cross, we were joined by a constable of that place and engaged a negro guide.

"After arriving at the camp where Young worked, we had to crawl along on our hands and knees through the brakes and marsh to a place where we could cover him as he passed. The men harrowed dirt from a pit some 200 yards from the place where it was dumped.

"We hid close to the place where he must pass and the guide stood, hat in hand, on the dump and watched. When Young passed the guide replaced his hat, the prearranged signal. We then sprang forward and covered the prisoner with Winchesters.

"One moment's forewarning would have been enough for him to have fled into impenetrable brakes where it would have been impossible ever to have hoped to find [him]."[1]

Mississippi Red surrendered without a fight. The lawmen returned to Houston with their prisoner on the evening of Sunday, December 29, 1911. The officers were literally fagged out from the trying ordeal. They shared the reward of $250 for the capture of Mississippi Red, but their expenses involved in the work ran much higher than that amount. Mississippi Red was subsequently tried and found guilty for killing Constable Isgit for which he was executed at the State Penitentiary in Huntsville in 1912.

A tent show came to Houston in the summer of 1912, bringing with it all sorts of bizarre people. Billed as the "Wild Man from Borneo," a wild and woolly negro in the company would continue his act after the tent show closed for the evening. Becoming uncontrollably drunk, this man pulled a knife and stabbed a negro woman in the hand. Officer Hamer was called and attempted to arrest the knife wielder, who made a break down the railroad track. Fearing to shoot owing to the many people about, there was nothing left for Hamer to do but get down to business and give chase. He finally outran the "wild man" in what the Houston *Press* called a "fair and square race, a feat not often accomplished by a white sprinter. The negro was relieved of a pistol and a pair of knucks and now languishes in the calaboose."[2]

In November 1912, Charles Smith escaped from the Huntsville State Penitentiary, where he had been sentenced from Harris County for a term of seven years on a charge of being implicated in the shooting of the yardmaster in the Houston Belt and Terminal Yards and the killing of a negro brakeman.

The shooting grew out of the burglary of several boxcars in the yard. The burglars were discovered by the yardman and the negro brakeman, and when they interfered both were shot, the brakeman being killed.

Soon after Smith's escape, news was received by Houston officers that the negro was in Houston, and efforts were made to capture him.

For several months news had reached the lawmen of boasts that Smith had made to the effect that he would not be captured alive.

Acting on a reliable underworld tip, Hamer, with special officers Anders and Matthews went to the First Ward in Houston, where they captured Smith without any resistance. Smith was returned to the penitentiary, where he served out the remainder of his seven-year term.[3]

In the first part of 1913, Hamer was responsible for the capture of a band of professional robbers, operating out of Houston. Again acting on underworld tips, Hamer was able to capture most of the members of this Mafia-led band. Recovering the stolen goods, Hamer learned that their operations extended in a wide radius from Houston. The gang would bring the stolen goods to organized "fences" in Houston who worked hand-in-glove with the thieves. Hamer let the stolen goods fall into the hands of these crooked peddlers. Thus trapping them, he and several other special policemen raided the fences, capturing seven of them. This resulted in prison sentences for all of the criminals apprehended. The Houston *Chronicle* reported: "It is a distinctive feather in Mr. Hamer's cap to have accomplished as much as he has, and it is confidently believed that before the end is announced he will be able to reveal more of the operations of this gang."[4]

Whenever things get too rough on crooks and the underworld, one begins to hear tales of police brutality, pistol whippings, and other attempts to stir the public against the defenders of the law. But occasionally the allegations are true, and Hamer became involved in one such instance while in Houston. He arrested a fellow officer for brutally pistol-whipping a man in front of the man's wife and children. There was some publicity about the incident, but Hamer's actions received the approval of Mayor Rice and the police department.

Early in 1913 the Houston Chief of Police, according to the Houston *Press*, charged that the special officers under Mayor Rice interfered with the functioning of the police department. The police chief hotly denied making the comment and went with Hamer to the newspaper office.

The police chief and Hamer argued with the author of the sensational story, who tried to pass the buck to his own boss, who passed it back to the writer. Before it was over there was a fight that lasted only a few seconds when Hamer slapped the reporter with his open hand.[5]

There were other incidents between various sections of the law enforcement agencies and the Houston newspapers. Politics came into the picture, and Hamer resigned in disgust.

Commenting on Hamer's resignation, a Houston newspaper stated: "He has the reputation of being quiet, steady, and a gentleman. He came to Houston and accepted employment as a Special Officer and no complaints against any of his actions as an officer or a citizen have ever been made."[6]

Hamer then went to Junction, in the Hill Country of Texas. While working there he tracked down a number of cattle and horse thieves, at the same time rounding up many wire cutters. During a brief visit to Navasota, Hamer captured three burglars who were wanted in Houston.[7]

Once, while chasing horse thieves, he called on the sheriff of Sutton County, a most effective law officer and a close friend of Hamer. This sheriff had a bad stutter. Hamer told him to watch out for the thieves, one of whom was heading through Sutton County.

Hamer set out after the man. When he reached the Allison Ranch, he found a telephone call from the sheriff. The conversation ran as follows:

Hello, Sheriff, what is it?"

"Hello, F-Frank . . . . F-F-Frank I-I-I g-got him."

"Y'did. Well, that's fine. Tell me about it."

"C-C-C-Come on in, F Frank, you c-can r-r-r-ride here b-b-b-before I c-c-can t-tell you."[8]

This same sheriff, on another occasion, was telling Frank about shooting a Mexican bandit:

"F-F-F-Frank, it was at n-n-n-night time, and I wasn't sure that I'd h-h-h-hit him f-f-f-for k-k-keeps, b-but i-i-i-in the morning, I-I-I-I found h-his body. H-H-He had b-b-been c-c-carrying a g-g-g-guitar, and m-m-my b-b-bullet hit him b-b-between the 'G' and 'B' strings."[9]

7

"Rangers, hell!
That's bandits a-comin'!"

In August 1914, World War I broke out in Europe. At that time the policy of the United States was isolationist, although American sympathies were naturally with the Allies. Worried by the probability of American involvement in the war, German Foreign Minister Dr. Alfred Zimmermann, conferred with Kaiser Wilhelm in regard to the possibility of embroiling the United States in a war with Mexico.

Mexico was in one of her usual "periods of unrest." Between 1911 and 1915 Mexico had no less than nine presidents, one of whom served a glorious total of 28 minutes. As a result of border troubles with Pancho Villa and considerable interference in Mexican affairs by President Woodrow Wilson, there was a strong anti-American feeling in Mexico. Usually this distaste for Americans was vented against "*los diablos*" Texans and their Rangers, but with the European war raging Mexico began to drift toward Germany. As a result, the "Plan de San Diego" was formulated in the jailhouse in Monterrey, Mexico, on January 6, 1915.

"The Plan de San Diego," a historian later wrote, "provided that on February 20, 1915, at two o'clock in the morning, the Mexicans were to arise in arms against the United States and proclaim their liberty and their independence of Yankee tyranny. At the same time, they would declare the independence of Texas, New Mexico, Arizona, Colorado, and California. The army would be the 'Liberating Army for

Races and People;' and the red flag with its white diagonal fringe would bear the inscription 'Equality and Independence.' Funds would be provided by levies on captured towns, and state governments would be set up in the state capitals."

"Every North American man over sixteen would be put to death as soon as his captors could extract from him all his funds or 'loans'; every stranger found armed should be executed regardless of race or nationality; no leader should enroll a stranger in the ranks unless he were Latin, negro, or Japanese. The Apaches of Arizona and other Indians were to receive every guarantee and have their lands returned to them."

"The first states were to be organized as an independent Mexican republic, which at an appropriate time would seek annexation to Mexico. When success had crowned the initial effort, six more states north of those named—evidently Oklahoma, Kansas, Nebraska, South Dakota, Wyoming, and Utah—were to be taken from the United States and given to the negroes who were to select a suitable banner for their republic. This buffer negro state would lie between the Mexicans and what one of the signers of the Plan called 'the damned big-footed creatures' of the north."[1]

The plan was discovered when a telegram from Zimmermann to his Minister to Mexico, Herr von Eckhardt, was intercepted by the Allies. It stated:

"We intend to begin on the first of February unrestricted submarine warfare. We shall endeavor in spite of this to keep the United States of America neutral. In the event of not succeeding, we make Mexico a proposal of alliance on the following basis: make war together, make peace together, generous financial support and an understanding on our part that Mexico is to reconquer the lost territory in Texas, New Mexico and Arizona. The settlement in detail is left to you. You will inform the President [of Mexico] of the above most secretly as soon as the outbreak of war with the United States of America is certain and add the suggestion that he should, on his initiative, invite Japan to immediate adherence and at the same time mediate between Japan and ourselves. Please call the President's attention to the fact that the ruthless employment of our submarines now offers the prospect of compelling in a few months to make peace.—Zimmermann."[2]

In a second telegram Zimmermann made it plain to Mexican President Venustiano Carranza that the alliance he was offering would dispose forever of the Monroe Doctrine and would form part of a permanent German–Mexican alliance.[3]

Meanwhile, however, people on the border knew nothing of the international skullduggery. But it became clear to the old-timers of the region that something was afoot.

As volatile Mexican residents along the Rio Grande were approached by various agents—German and others—and led to believe that they were being deprived of their rights, raids and banditry increased. Strange rumors began to float through South Texas. Charles Armstrong, who lived on the border, stated that the people "could feel that something mysterious and terrible was impending, but they could not guess what it was. The Mexicans—the good Mexicans—felt it but could not express it. Something was wrong. Shrugs. Gestures. Strange horsemen riding through the brush. The grapevine of the border, transmitting strange messages among ignorant but simple-hearted and kindly people. Mexicans who had always been tractable became timid or sullen."[4]

Led by Luis de la Rosa and Aniceto Pizana, organized and usually well-armed bands began to raid the ranches between Del Rio and Brownsville.

Needing experienced men to cope with the situation, Capt E. H. Smith, commander of Texas Ranger Company C, approached Hamer in March of 1915. He convinced Hamer to rejoin the Rangers and help the small band protect several hundred miles of seething border. Hamer signed up at Del Rio on March 29, 1915, and was described in the enlistment form as: "Francis A. Hamer, 31 years, 12 days old, 6 feet 3 inches tall, brown hair, blue eyes."[5]

Throughout the spring and summer Hamer rode with Company C, patrolling the Rio Grande. The Rangers intercepted numerous bands of raiders and bandidos, and yet—even though there was plenty of action—there were no major uprisings or invasions. Higher authorities still felt that one company of Texas Rangers was sufficient to defend the border from Mexican invasion. Besides, some U.S. Cavalry units were stationed nearby should any real trouble arise.

Trouble did arise, but in an unexpected form. Tom Lea tells part of the story: "During the first days of August, 1915, a formidable band of Mexican horsemen rode the brush more than fifty miles north of Brownsville. When their presence on the Sauz division of the King Ranch was reported to Caesar Kleberg, who was at Kingsville for the weekend, he telephoned to the rangers at Brownsville and to the Army command at Fort Brown, requesting immediate help for the handful of cowboys, headed by foreman Tom Tate, who were charged with the protection of the southern end of the ranch. Early in the afternoon of August 8 a special train left Brownsville, bound for Norias. It carried an Army captain, a squad of eight troopers from the 12th Cavalry, two Texas Ranger captains, several rangers [among whom was Hamer] and a group of local peace officers. Upon their arrival at Norias, they found King Ranch horses ready and waiting. The whole armed party, except for the squad of troopers, mounted and rode southeastward, with Tom Tate and several King Ranch cowhands, looking for a fight in the direction of the Sauz pastures where the Mexicans had been reported."

"An hour and a half after the special train's departure, the regular afternoon northbound had left Brownsville. Aboard it for the ride, stirred by curiosity over the purposes of the special train ahead, were three adventuresome customs inspectors—Portus Gay, Joe Taylor, Marcus Hinds, and their friend Gordon Hill, a deputy sheriff of Cameron County—all of them armed, all of them ready for any excitement they might encounter up the line. They had it."[6]

Another younger man was with the group, Luke Snow. Luke's brother, retired Texas Game Warden Bob Snow, relates what followed:

"After supper Hines walked up on the front part of the porch and said, 'I see the Rangers coming back. They didn't meet those bandits.' Luke looked out and said, 'Rangers, hell! That's bandits a-comin'!' They looked around and saw the whole surrounding skyline filled with men—bandits—on horseback. Portus Gay and the soldiers lay down behind the railroad track alongside Snow and Gordon Hill, Deputy Sheriff of Cameron County. Marcus Hines got behind a barrel that was full of water in a corner of the yard. He had a 10-gauge lever-action Winchester shotgun, and the other boys had .30-30's. The bandits formed a line, and came running horseback. They had a bull-proof fence along the east side of the railroad track, made out of big heavy net wire with smooth wire above it, but the bandits didn't know about it. They run up horseback, and the soldiers opened fire and old Marcus Hines began shooting with his 10-gauge shotgun. Its noise nearly deafened the men on the left. When the first bunch of bandits hit the wire, their horses stopped and they bunched up there."

The shotgun and the rifles had the proper effect.

"It got so hot that the bandits fell back to regroup, leaving six or eight dead men behind, along with several dead and wounded horses. Luke later told me about these horses screaming. He'd never heard a horse make that kind of noise before. During the first onslaught, one soldier was hit in the heel, knocking his military shoe off and tearing the heel up. While the bandits were falling back, the other soldiers started their wounded comrade back in to the building. Two or three of the bandits shot, hitting this same soldier in the leg below the knee as they were carrying him back in the building."

"During the lull after the first attack, Marcus Hines got to looking at his 'fort'. There was water running out of the barrel from three bullet holes. He said, 'I'm a big old son-of-a-so-and-so; I'm gonna get better cover than this.'"

"He went over and lay behind the railroad tracks with the others, who told him:

"'We are sure glad you brought that old cannon along side of us, because it already has us deafened from behind'."

"The bandits charged again, this time some of those in front falling over the bull-proof fence. These bandits were quickly dispatched by the defenders, who killed seventeen of them altogether. Again and again the bandits charged, only to lose more of their number by the accurate fire of the defenders. Finally, at about eight-thirty that evening, the bandits retired, leaving the exhausted defenders of Norias alone."[7]

About nine-thirty the main force of lawmen rode up, having failed to make any contact with the Mexicans. They captured Tomas Rinconesco, or Manuel Rincones, as some accounts have it, a young Mexican who was with the raiders. Mortally wounded, he told the names of all the raiders he knew. It turned out quite a few were from the Texas side of the border, mostly from the Brownsville area. Checking off the Mexicans who had been killed, the Rangers had a list of most of the surviving participants.

Stationing what men they could round up from immigration and customs service at key spots along the river to keep any of the retreating Mexicans from crossing the border, the Rangers searched out the participants. An unknown but substantial number of "suicides" occurred during the next day or two, and the list grew shorter.

As Bob Snow laconically put it, "The Rangers got rough with those people, but they had to."[8] The raids ceased along the lower Rio Grande, as a result, only to intensify farther north on the river. The Texas Rangers followed the raids.

It was no-holds-barred warfare between the Rangers and the bandidos. One of the Mexicans' favorite tricks, for example, was that of pretending to surrender. Whenever surrounded by Rangers, one of the bandits would wave a white sheet or piece of cloth and yell, "Señor Texans, don't shot, don't shot! We surrender! We geev up!"

Then, as the Rangers stepped up toward the Mexican, the still-hidden bandits would shoot them down. Thereafter, the only death that occurred when a white flag was waved was that of the waver.[9]

Another big raid was made on the Brite Ranch in the Sierra Viega Mountains south of Valentine, Texas. Between fifty and a hundred Mexicans captured the ranch, held some of the occupants prisoner, slaughtered a number of others, hanged three luckless travelers who happened by, stole everything of value, and leisurely began to drive the ranch's livestock back to Mexico.

Hamer and about ten members of Company C, hearing of the killings, set out after the bandits. Hamer and his men followed them to the border, keeping out of sight. The Mexicans crossed and entered their stronghold of Candelia, immediately beginning a wild victory celebration. Late that night the eleven Rangers "surrounded" Candelia and opened fire. The drunken Mexicans returned the fire with about as much success as their grandparents had at San Jacinto. When the shooting ended, not one live Mexican could be found. The population of Candelia dropped sharply that night.[10]

8

"The Lone Ranger of the Rio Grande."

"THE EMBARGO OF ARMS TO MEXICO IS ON," bannered newspaper headlines on October 14, 1915.[1] The United States had officially recognized the Mexican government of Venustiano Carranza over those of Villa and other revolutionaries. Appreciating Carranza's rejection of a German–Mexican alliance, President Woodrow Wilson proclaimed an all-out embargo of arms and ammunitions shipments into Mexico, thereby assuring the security of the Carranza regime.

All law enforcement agencies on the Rio Grande were ordered to intensify their efforts to halt smuggling of arms and supplies to the forces of Villa and other Mexican revolutionary bands. The Texas Rangers were dispersed along the border with written orders to enforce the embargo to the fullest and to allow no guns or munitions whatsoever to pass into Mexico.

For awhile the Rangers were able to slow down the flow of arms. Then trouble arose in an unexpected quarter. A strange verbal order was sent down from higher state headquarters: "Ease off the embargo," the Rangers were instructed. "Let the munitions pass into Mexico, but continue to put up a show of trying to stop them."[2]

This order was a great blow to the Rangers because many of the arms taken into Mexico were used by bandits to raid the American side of the border. "Hamer suspected that somebody in Austin had been bribed," H. M. Mason reports, or had some political interests in Mexican affairs. Hamer however, did know "that the law was the law, and he intended to keep right on enforcing it."[3]

Hamer always felt that a lawman's toughest fights came not with outlaws or common criminals but with crooks in places of authority. Texas had had its share of murderers, thieves, and bad men, but it has had more than its share of crooked politicians. Hamer's biggest battles throughout his career would be with crooked politicians and dishonest political appointees.

Hamer sent word back that he intended to continue to enforce President Wilson's order for an embargo. If the state's powers-that-be wanted him to do differently, they could send the order in writing or dismiss him from the Rangers. He received no reply and continued to perform his duty.

Then the retaliation that he expected began to take place: Gradually, a few at a time, the other Rangers were withdrawn from border duty. Hamer found himself covering an ever-increasing area, nearly always alone. Within a few months Hamer was the only Texas Ranger along the Rio Grande from Brownsville nearly to the Big Bend. It became clear that higher officialdom in Texas not only intended to ignore the embargo but hoped to get Hamer out of the way in the process.

It was, of course, an impossible task for one man to guard such a large area alone; and the chances were less than slim for a lone Texas Ranger to stay alive in the midst of the hundreds of bandits and revolutionaries who depended on smuggled American arms for their existence. Hamer found himself playing right into the hands of a political machine that he would fight in Texas politics for the next twenty years.

Undaunted, as usual, Hamer found a solution: if he could not patrol the South Texas border all by himself, he would cross the border, join the Mexican police, and patrol the North Mexican border instead. He crossed the Rio Grande at Jimenez and met with the captain of the rurales. Suggesting that he throw in his experience with theirs, Hamer outlined his plan for protecting the border. The rurales' chief, who time and again had been outfoxed by the cunning of the bandits and Villa revolutionaries, was only too glad to have the *muy macho* Ranger on his side.

"As a result of this conference," Webb wrote, "Hamer crossed the Rio Grande and became the virtual head of a large squad of Mexican soldiers who combed ninety miles of border. When stolen property or stock was located and identified, the possessors were invited to back up against an adobe wall about thirty feet from a military firing squad, and the stolen goods were assembled and returned to their owners in Texas."[4]

Hamer was alone in Del Rio one day when he received a reliable tip that some horse thieves were about to cross the border into Mexico. Hamer sent word to his rurale cohort and rode alone to the intended crossing point. Concealing his horse far back in the rocks, Hamer crawled to a point on a nearby hill where he could watch the border. Shortly, ten men rode by, driving some horses ahead of them that they had stolen on the American side of the Rio Grande. They crossed the river into Mexico and proceeded up to a nearby canyon. After fifteen minutes had passed, Hamer heard a single shot, then a volley. A short time later the rurale leader rode out into the river and called to Hamer, who went to meet him.

"I appreciate your information, *amigo*" said the rurale. "All of the *cabrones* are dead, and here are your horses."[5]

The lone ranger of the Rio Grande accepted the horses with a grin and headed them north to be returned to their owners.

With his company of rurales, Hamer chased smugglers, fought bandits, recovered stolen arms, and maintained law and order along the border of two nations.

9

"I invited him to get up and fight me face to face."

In 1916 the Texas Cattle Raisers Association requested that the Rangers release a man to work on detached service with them to apprehend cattle rustlers who were still operating in some parts of the state. Captain John H. Rogers recommended Hamer:

"Mr. Hamer," Rogers wrote to the secretary of the association, "is one of the most active officers I have ever known. He is absolutely void of fear, and while he is not an educated man, he is bright and intelligent, very industrious and a splendid detective. He was raised and grew up in the West, and when I first enlisted him he was a typical cowboy. . . . The criminal and more dangerous and hazardous the work, the better he likes it. . . . I have never recommended a man for this position that I recommend so heartily and unqualifiedly as I do Mr. Hamer. . . . He is a live wire beyond a doubt, and the lawless element stand in awe of him wherever he has worked."[1]

Hamer accepted and began to investigate cases of cattle and horse stealing throughout the state.

During this period, Hamer's younger brother Harrison was working on the ranch of W. A. "Bill" Johnson, a prominent rancher and banker in Snyder, Texas. While investigating a case south of Snyder one day, Hamer decided to pay a visit to his brother. At the Snyder Ranch he met Johnson's attractive daughter, Gladys.

The young lady was impressed by the tall, smiling lawman. "He was daring and handsome," she recalls. "The Lord seemed always to be tapping him on the shoulder."[2]

The attraction was mutual, and on May 12, 1917, Hamer and Gladys Johnson were married in New Orleans, Louisiana.[3] Beginning a thirty-eight-year marriage that was to last until Hamer's death, they settled in Snyder, with two daughters from Gladys's previous marriage, Beverly and Helen Sims. Hamer continued his work for the cattle raisers association.

Land disputes have probably brought on more violent feuds in Texas than any other cause. Such a dispute arose when a group of men attempted to take over some of Mr. Johnson's land, and one of the Johnson men was killed. The killer was arrested and trial was set in Baird, Texas. Hamer began to gather evidence against the man and was the state's expert witness for the ensuing trial. The killer's attorney, according to Harrison Kinney, "weighed the evidence against his client and told the man's family their only choice for acquittal was to kill the state's expert witness, Frank Hamer. It was common enough advice on the part of counsel in those days, but acting on it, everybody agreed, would be a mite ticklish in this case."[4]

Several men were hired for the job of assassinating Hamer. One was a former sheriff and ranger named Gee McMeans. Another was H. E. Phillips, and the third was Bob Higgdon, "considered the deadliest gunman then roaming the southwest."[5]

W. G. Clark was hired, as well as two notorious El Paso gunmen. Clark swore in a deposition on June 14, 1917:

"W. G. Clark, of lawful age, being first duly sworn on his oath, deposes and says, that Felix R. Jones, on or about the first of May, 1917, in Abilene, Tex. partially made a trade with me to kill Bill Johnson of Snyder, Texas . . . for a consideration of $4,000.00, which was to be paid to me by T. A. Morrison . . . and further stated that when I killed Johnson, that I would be forced to kill another man by the name of Hamer, as they were always together and in case that I did have to kill Hamer, that I would be well paid for that also and that the said T. A. Morrison was slated himself to kill the present Sheriff of Scurry County, Texas, his name being Merrill. And then it was also understood that in case that I did not have to kill Hamer, that T. A. Morrison was to kill for himself. . . . The said

Morrison also stated that the thing to do and would have to be done, was to kill Bill Johnson before the next term of Court. On Wednesday, May 23rd, Morrison called me up from Colorado City from Abilene by phone and told me to come there that night. I knew what this meant, as he had agreed to get up the actual money and have it in his possession.

I went over there Wednesday night and he showed me the $4,000.00 in fifty dollar bills he was to give me."[6]

The El Paso gunmen also planned to go to Snyder, but just before leaving, a $10,000 reward was offered for the arrest of one of the two, and the other turned him in to collect the reward.[7] McMeans, Phillips, and Higgdon had Hamer and Johnson all to themselves.

Higgdon even had S. D. Meyers, a well-known leathersmith, make him three special holsters to allow for his lightning draw.[8]

The killers were also after Harrison. McMeans walked up to Harrison one day in the lobby of a hotel in Post City and kicked at his feet, trying to egg him into a fight. McMeans had two pistols on, while Harrison's guns were upstairs in his room. Harrison managed to hold his anger and keep still, and McMeans went away laughing.[9] A friend of the Hamers', H. L. Roberson, saw what happened and called Frank. As Hamer himself later related, Roberson "informed me that my brother was liable to be killed." Riding directly to the ranch of the killer, Hamer said: "I informed the bunch, which was headed by a man by the name of McMeans, that if anyone murdered my brother that they would pay dearly for it and immediately thereafter the hatred of the entire bunch was directed toward me. McMeans openly boasted the fact that he would kill me on sight, as witnesses from Fort Worth to El Paso testified. I did not know McMeans."[10]

Early one morning in September 1917, McMeans and several other hirelings hid in ambush along the route from the Johnson place into Snyder. As Johnson's car drove toward the spot where they were hidden, the car suddenly stopped and Hamer jumped out, his rifle blazing. The four ambushers broke and ran as fast as they could. It turned out that Hamer and Mr. Johnson had seen a large gray wolf and Hamer had jumped out to kill it, having no idea an ambush was awaiting them.[11]

By this time Hamer and Harrison had had enough. Driving on into Snyder they looked for their assailants.

"Look over yonder next to that cafe," Hamer muttered.

His brother looked and saw two of the gang. Harrison described what happened:

"So we sat down there and directly they came out of that place and went straight across to the First National Bank, and just about the time they got on the sidewalk, Frank said, 'Let's go.' I said, 'AH right!' We got up and went meetin' 'em. I was on the side next of the building and Frank was on the outside. Frank said, 'Which one do you want?' I answered, 'It don't make a damn to me, take your pick.' Frank named the one that he wanted. I said, 'All right, I'll take the other.' So we met them, and when we got right up to them, they began to speak: 'Hello, hello there,' one of them said two or three times. Frank knocked one of them down and the other threw up his hands and said, 'Don't hit me, don't hit me!' I grabbed him by the collar and shoved him up against the abutment of that First National Bank building, and smashed his nose and his lips and all. Frank was jest stompin' the hell out of his man. Frank finally got him up and told him to 'Pull out that pistol you've got in your pocket and use it!' But the man wouldn't pull it, and Frank then kicked him plumb out in the street. Hell, he wouldn't do nothin', so Frank turned him loose, and I let mine go too."[12]

Despite the threats and attempted murders, Hamer rode to Baird on October 1, 1917, and testified in the trial. Hamer later wrote: "On the morning of October 1, 1917, I was a witness in district court at Baird, Texas, and the case was continued. While making preparations to return to Snyder, Texas, a bunch of men came to me and advised me not to go through Sweetwater, Texas [which was on the road to Snyder], as McMeans and others were in Sweetwater for the purpose of murdering me."[13]

Hamer shrugged off the warnings and drove on toward Snyder. As he passed through Abilene, however, he noticed something out of the corner of his eye. A lawyer friend of McMeans was staring down out of his second-story office at the Hamers with a smile on his face. He calmly strapped on an extra pistol, a .44 caliber Smith and Wesson "triple-lock" revolver. His .45, "Old Lucky," was on the other hip, and they drove on to Sweetwater.

Hamer stated: "Immediately after entering the city limits of Sweetwater which was about 1:30 PM October 1, 1917, I had a puncture and drove into a garage which was located on the South-East corner of the square of Sweetwater, Texas.

I walked from my car to the office of the garage to get someone to fix my tire."[14] Harrison and Emmett Johnson went across an alley to use the toilet. Gladys remained in the car. Everyone seemed to sense that trouble was in the air.

As Frank stepped out of the office, McMeans jumped out from behind a door and shot Hamer point-blank, yelling: "I've got you now, God damn you!"

The bullet drove Hamer's watch chain deep into his left shoulder, incapacitating his normal gun hand. He grappled with his other hand for McMeans's gun, knocking it down as it fired again; the shot tearing into Hamer's leg.

At this moment occurred one of the most uncanny events of Hamer's career. Hamer, attacked by surprise and shot twice at point-blank range with a powerful .45 automatic by a man less than four feet away, stepped right up to McMeans and took hold of the end his gun barrel. Level-headed and quick-thinking even at a time like this, Hamer amid all the shooting had not heard the last shell from McMeans' pistol hit the wooden sidewalk. Hamer knew the gun had jammed, so he wrenched the pistol away and began to cuff McMeans with his open hand.

Meanwhile, another gun battle was raging beside them. Gladys, straining to see what was happening to her husband, noticed H. E. Phillips creeping across the street toward Hamer's back with a shotgun. She yelled, then picked up a small automatic pistol from the front seat and opened fire. Phillips ducked back behind a car. Every time he attempted to move forward, Gladys would fire. In desperation Phillips swung his shotgun around at her, but did not fire, wanting to save his ammunition for Hamer. Finally, Gladys ran out of shells and Phillips crossed the street just as Hamer had closed with McMeans.[15]

Hamer, himself, wrote about what happened next. "Another man, who was unknown to me, came running toward me with an automatic shot gun—the man I was clinched with jerked loose from me and the other man fired at my head with the shot gun, the muzzle of the gun being about three feet from my head, cutting my hat brim off."[16]

"I got him! I got him!" Phillips yelled. Then he saw Hamer shaking his head from the concussion of the gun and realized that the big man was still on his knees. Terrified, both men ran to their car.

Hamer, wounded severely and with his gun hand useless, headed after them. McMeans, says Hamer, "grabbed a pump shot gun from his car and attempted to open fire on me again—I then pulled my pistol [the Smith and Wesson] and shot him through the heart, killing him instantly—he fell on the sidewalk out of sight from where I was standing—I staggered to the front door and the stranger who had shot my hat brim off with his shot gun was hunkered down by the side of the dead man with his shot gun across his lap—I invited him to get up and fight me face to face, but he immediately broke and ran down the sidewalk with his shot gun in his hand—I called for him to turn around, not caring to shoot him in the back."[17]

But Phillips had had enough of Hamer and never paused. Harrison, who had been caught with his pants down, ran up at this moment and leveled his rifle at the retreating figure, but Hamer knocked the barrel up just as he shot.

"Leave him," Hamer said, as Phillips ran into a cafe.

"Frank didn't want me to shoot him in the back," Harrison recalled, "but I wasn't thinking about that after what he'd done. I was gonna kill that son-of-a-bitch, but then he ran into that side door. I quit Frank and went [after him], and Phillips just flattened himself up against the door, which was a big old swinging door. I couldn't see anything; I just stood there ready for him, and he never did show up. When he didn't show I turned and went back outside to Frank. The deputy had come across the street and arrested Phillips."[18]

Another police officer down the street picked up a woman with a paper bag full of ten dollar bills, totaling five thousand dollars—the payoff money for murdering Hamer.[19]

A county grand jury happened to be in session across the street and the entire jury watched the whole fight with a bird's-eye view from the window. As the doctor was sewing Hamer up in the courtroom, the grand jury reconvened, absolved Hamer on the spot, and ruled that no indictment was indicated. They made a point of complimenting him on not shooting Phillips in the back.[20]

That evening Bob Higgdon arrived in Sweetwater on the train, according to Harrison Kinney, "in time to see McMeans' shrouded figure being toted off to the funeral parlor. He misunderstood who was under the sheet and put on quite a show of disappointment, yelling that he'd planned to kill Frank Hamer and that McMeans hadn't the decency to wait for him. Somebody finally told him that the job was still open—Frank Hamer was still in town. Gee McMeans hadn't hogged all the glory after all."

"Higgdon growled and grumbled for a time, fingering the special holster thonged to his thigh, but finally he allowed that it wouldn't do to take on a wounded man, not a decent thing at all, and when the next train came in, he got on it. Plenty of people still wanted Hamer killed, but Higgdon seems to have quit that whole section of the country. Word drifted back that he'd wound up in California and wasn't wearing his holsters any more."[21]

10

"A giant of a man . . . and as talkative as an oyster."

When Hamer had sufficiently recovered from his wounds, he and Gladys journeyed to the West Coast for an extended vacation. While visiting Universal City in Hollywood they met actor Tom Mix. A strong friendship immediately developed between the Texas Ranger and the cowboy star. Mix spent several days with the Hamers, taking them around the various sets where different movies were being filmed. On a western set, Mix commented: "Watch that so-called cowboy yonder try to get on that horse. He don't even know how to mount. He'd just as soon mount on the right side as the left—that's what we've gotta put up with around here."[1]

Mix tried to get Hamer to stay in Hollywood and become a Western actor. He said Hamer had the looks, the bearing, and the athletic ability to become a great cowboy star. Because Mix and Bill Hart were the only two actors in Hollywood who could ride a horse without falling off, Hamer could probably outdo them all.

Gladys interposed, however, even though Hamer had no serious intentions of staying. Mix and Hamer remained close friends, and more than once during the next fifteen years Mix came to Texas to visit Hamer. Mix said he liked to watch the way Hamer walked and talked, but Hamer only laughed, saying Mix had seen too many of his own movies.[2]

Another writer, years later, commented on Hamer's likeness to the Hollywood ideal: "It's embarrassing to describe Frank Hamer in these days of TV westerns.

One can hear about him and examine his photographs, and then one realizes that Hamer is the real character all TV casting directors are driving for. He was a gentleman and always very nice to the ladies. He was big, strong, and silent but he didn't like people who questioned him, and he was able to communicate his dislike while doffing his hat and saying 'Yes, Ma'am.' A lady tourist spotted Hamer in the coffee shop of the Austin Hotel and asked him why he always wore black suits. Hamer replied, It happens to suit my character, Ma'am'."[3]

A newspaperman once wrote about Hamer: "He was a giant of a man, moon-faced, always in boots, and as talkative as an oyster."[4]

Hamer told Mix he did not like the Hollywood way of glorifying killing, nor the way it always had the bad man drawing first. Mix was amazed at Hamer's shooting ability, even though Hamer didn't shoot from the hip. Writer Kinney states:

"Hamer often said shooting from the hip was a lot of damned Hollywood nonsense and risky for bystanders as well as for the man doing the shooting. He was known to take careful aim at shoulder level with Old Lucky while a bad man fanned shots at him from all those contorted positions readers of western pulps assumes to be deadliest.

"Once his Austin friend, Victor Friedrichs, asked Hamer if he'd ever shot from the hip."

"Once in a while," Hamer conceded, "the man I was shooting at was so close I didn't have room to raise my gun and point it properly."[5]

Hamer hardly ever wore a cartridge belt, saying that any man who got himself into a position where he needed all those shots was "just plain guilty of sloppy peace-officering."[6]

To all of which Mix reluctantly agreed, knowing nevertheless that cowboy movies would never change their image of the typical cowboy "hero."

So Hamer and Gladys returned to Texas, driving leisurely through Utah, Yellowstone, Colorado, and New Mexico, while Hamer regained his strength. By the time the Hamers reached Snyder, Hamer was as strong as he had ever been and itching for action.

During the trip, on April 11, 1918, Gladys gave birth to the Hamers' first son, Frank A. Hamer, Jr. This new addition, like his father, became a Texas Ranger, serving on the private staff of Governor Allen Shivers, and then serving for many years as a Texas Game Warden. One of Gladys's two daughters became

Mrs. Verne McMullan, wife of a rancher, and the other married Albert Benson, a prominent architect.

After settling Gladys and the new baby and getting the girls in school, Hamer returned to the Texas Rangers. He began work on October 1, 1918, in the company of Captain W. W. Taylor at Brownsville.[7] He also worked with Captain Charles Stevens.

As World War I drew toward a close, prohibition was in its infancy. No whiskey had been manufactured in the United States since September 8, 1917, and thirsty Americans had to depend on their neighborhood bootlegger to supply any hard liquor they wished to consume.[8] As a result, bootlegging flourished, adding impetus to an already-rising crime rate. Much of the whiskey consumed at that time was smuggled across the border from Mexico. Tequila—that fiery-hot liquor distilled from the mezcal plant—could be bought in Mexico for fifty cents a quart; and rum did not cost much more. These and other types of liquor were smuggled across the Rio Grande into the United States by enterprising bootleggers. Horses and burros were used to carry their illicit cargo some 75 miles into Texas, where automobiles and trucks would pick up the booze and speed it northward. At the final destination, this whiskey would bring anywhere from eight to fifteen dollars per quart.

The Texas Rangers were faced with stopping this traffic, despite the adverse publicity that it aroused among a large segment of the state. Owen P. White, a noted Southwestern author, wrote:

"Just imagine if you can, you who know Texas, and who know how much of its greatness the Lone Star State owes to such men as Jim Gillette, John B. Jones, Dick Ware, George W. Baylor, and a host of others; just imagine any of them going around and patting their fellow citizens on the hip in search of a pint of liquor. They wouldn't have done it! They were real men who had real jobs with traditions behind them, and just consider for a moment, what a disastrous effect it would have had, not only upon those traditions, but upon the life and happiness of the people as well, if those grand old fellows who fought Apaches, hung horse thieves, captured train robbers, and exterminated cattle rustlers had made it a part of their daily business to snoop and spy and arrest their neighbor just because he was the proud and happy possessor of a bottle of good whiskey."[9]

Once more Hamer was faced with the choice of ignoring the law of the land or enforcing a law in the face of its general unpopularity. The Lord, indeed, "seemed always to be tapping him on the shoulder."

Nestled in a cruel curve of the Rio Grande, Tomate Bend was, and still is, one of the most bloody points on the river. Located near Brownsville, this frequently blind crossing abounds with thick, semitropical undergrowth, providing excellent cover for wetbacks, smugglers, and other underworld denizens.

Acting on a hot tip, Cameron County Sheriff W. T. Vann notified Ranger Headquarters that a band of smugglers planned to cross the river at Tomate Bend with a load of liquor on October 4, 1918. The leader of the band was a notorious bootlegger and bandit, Incarnacion Delgado. Sheriff Vann, Captain Taylor, Hamer, and a few other Rangers made plans to intercept them.

Just before leaving Ranger Headquarters to intercept the smugglers, Hamer walked into the room of another Ranger, Sergeant Delbert Timberlake, and found him in the act of burning his personal letters and packing his baggage.

"What in hell are you doing, Tim?" Hamer asked.

"Frank, I've got the feeling that I won't be needing this stuff any more after tonight," replied Timberlake.

"Aw, stop that nonsense," argued Hamer, "nothing's going to happen to you tonight that hasn't happened in the past. That Delgado is the one who's going to get it."

"I just can't help it, Pancho, I've got a funny notion that things are going to end for me down at Tomate."

Sheriff Vann and Hamer had a minor dispute as the lawmen rode toward Tomate Bend. Vann insisted on trying to arrest the band without shooting, even though it would be in the middle of the night. Hamer disagreed.

"Sheriff, you know that sidewinder Delgado isn't going to surrender as long as he has a chance to shoot his way out of the trap. If you try to arrest him, you'll get yourself shot for sure."

"I'm sorry, Frank," the sheriff replied, "but I'm not going to take any chance of shooting an innocent person."

"Now, what in hell is an innocent person going to be doing down at Tomate at this time of night?" asked Hamer.

The matter was dropped and the lawmen concealed themselves in the brush along the smugglers' route. Hamer, who preferred to work alone against such odds, noticed that the others had foolishly brought shotguns instead of rifles. Timberlake said, "The way I feel tonight, one gun will do me about as much good as another."

After a long wait, the lawmen heard what sounded like the bleat of a goat, the signal between Delgado and his confederates on the American side of the border. Sheriff Vann jumped up and walked toward the sound, commanding: "Alto! Halt!"

Immediately Delgado stood up and fired a shot at the Rangers and the sheriff. The bullet ricocheted off a rock and hit Timberlake in the stomach. The sheriff fired twice with his shotgun, but Delgado was too far away. Using only the single flash from Delgado's pistol to guide him, Hamer fired his .25-caliber Remington rifle, pulling the trigger so fast that the flashes looked like the jet flame from the torch burner used by cattlemen to burn thorns off prickly pears.

"Good God!" one awed Ranger exclaimed. "Look at Frank use that pear burner on him!"[10]

Not sure where the bandit was, the other lawmen held their fire. The other bandits had splashed back across the Rio Grande. Hamer lowered his rifle, struck a match, and led the men to the body of Delgado, sprawled across a large cactus plant, still clutching his pistol in one hand and spare cartridges in the other.

One bullet had hit his hand and two more had hit him squarely in the chest.

For years after this night, fellow Rangers would say that Hamer used "Old Lucky" during the day but always took his pear burner with him at night.[11]

Timberlake was taken to a Brownsville hospital, where in his final minutes, he asked to talk to Hamer. As Webb later reported the conversation: "Pancho," said the wounded man, "there's no chance for me, is there?"

"No, Tim, there's not a chance for you."

"Did he get away?" asked the man on the bed.

"No."

"That helps a whole lot," said the Timberlake.

Then a tremor passed over him and Hamer pulled the white sheet over the face of his companion and went out to a group of fellow officers who stood by the window.

"Well, he's cashed in," he informed them.

"Hamer," said one of the officers, "if we had followed your advice, things might have been different. We made a mistake."

"Yes," he assented, nodding to the white sheet that could be seen through the window, "and there is your mistake."[12]

Hamer was promoted to Ranger Sergeant, a position he held for more than a year, his group protecting the border as no other law force could ever do.

One morning during 1919 Hamer and some other Rangers in his company were treated to an amusing spectacle along the border. This was still a time of unrest in Mexico, and revolutions against President Carranza were taking place. On patrol along the river near Del Rio, Hamer and his company heard firing across the border.

Concealing their horses, the Rangers crept behind some boulders which afforded them both cover and concealment but allowed them to have a clear view of the Mexican side of the Rio Grande. The Rangers watched as opposing armed Mexican forces, most likely Carranzistas and sympathizers of rebel General José Gonzalo Escobar, were hard at work trying to eliminate one another. For almost the entire day the Rangers watched the battle through field glasses.

First, the Carranzistas, located behind a hill, would run out and wildly charge their opponents, blowing bugles and shouting furiously.

The rebels would defend their position just as furiously, blowing their bugles and shouting their own slogans and curses. Then the rebels would countercharge, and the Carranzistas would defend. Both sides would take frequent rest periods to reorganize and, likely, to recover their voices.

At one point the leader of the Carranzistas charged his horse right past the rebels' lines and down into the middle of the Rio Grande. Waving his sword and screaming curses, he tried vainly to force his mount to turn and charge again at the enemy. All three groups—Carranzistas, rebels, and Rangers—paused to watch the officer as he swore at his horse, only to be ingloriously pitched head first into the shallow muddy waters. He crawled to shore and scrambled to his forces, whereupon the battle raged once more.

The Rangers took turns counting as many of the shots that were fired as they could, stopping at two thousand. Late in the afternoon both sides quitted their positions and apparently went home for supper. The only casualty during the entire day occurred just before the end of the battle, when the Carranzista leader, to regain lost face, shot his horse.[13]

11

"There was a gunfight for 236 straight nights!"

Throughout 1919 Hamer and his men worked around Del Rio, chasing thieves, rumrunners, and dope peddlers. The war ended, and except for bootleggers, the border began to become a safe place to live. Just before the end of the war, however, the Ranger force had been increased from its small, closely knit group to a thousand men.

With this new law, men of questionable competence and honesty began to join the force. What galled Hamer the most was the wholesale appointment by the governor of political lackeys and henchmen. Webb wrote: "The Ranger service was also affected by the fact that the state was split politically into Ferguson and anti-Ferguson factions. Both factions used the Rangers for political purposes at a time when the force really had a great opportunity for distinguished service. O. B. Colquitt seems to have been responsible for introducing the spoils system into the Ranger Force, but [James] Ferguson and [William] Hobby went further in sinking the Rangers in the mire, and their vicious policy has been followed by succeeding governors without exception."[1]

Bill Sterling, one of the best of the Texas Ranger captains, wrote in later life: "One day in Laredo I met a charming lady, wife of a Chicago railroad executive, who was stopping over on her way to Mexico. Her first words to me were, 'I have just had a childhood illusion shattered. I've always wanted to meet a real Texas Ranger and on his native soil. I've just seen the captain stationed here. Imagine my disappointment and chagrin when I met, not the tall, tanned rider I had always visualized, but a flabby, pasty-faced bartender.' I hung my head as any good Texan would and tried to explain to the disillusioned lady that he was a Ferguson Ranger, and a typical representative of that administration."[2]

Disgusted with the turn of events, Hamer resigned in April 1920, and joined the U.S. prohibition service. It was unpopular work, but in view of the fact that most of the more notorious outlaws of the day were bootleggers as well, it gave him leeway for law enforcement that the Ranger force's political situation did not.

He reported for duty on April 11 and was assigned to the El Paso area. Once his son Frank, Jr., asked him about his El Paso days, and Hamer told him: "El Paso was one of the toughest towns I'd ever been in. There was a gunfight for 236 straight nights!"[3]

Shortly after arriving in El Paso, Hamer and other "prohis," as they were called, were sent to nearby Anapra, New Mexico, to assist Customs Officer Joe Davenport in a battle with seven whiskey runners. Davenport and two others had hidden near the Mexico–Texas–New Mexico border to surprise the rumrunners, and spotted a whole caravan. The El Paso *Times* reported:

"The caravan consisted of six mounted men in front, followed by pack horses, and about 200 yards in the rear was a pack train of burros, carrying the contraband. This burro train was in charge of one man, who followed, riding a burro. 'When the horsemen arrived within about twenty feet of us, I called to them to 'halt'," stated Inspector Davenport, in reporting the affair. "I called to them that we were Customs Officers and had no sooner done so than there was a volley from the smugglers. One of the first shots struck me and I fell to the ground but managed to get my gun in action. All of us were shooting by this time and the smugglers were making back toward the border. They made an effort to stampede the burro train, but did not succeed. A telephone message was sent to the Customs Office in El Paso and Inspector J. D. Reeder sent out a detachment to assist the Inspectors. . . ."[4]

Hamer and some others hurried to the scene and the smugglers retreated back across the border, leaving 407 quarts of tequila and 22 pints of whiskey, as well as their pack animals.

In the fall of 1920 a spectacular daytime gun battle took place at Cordova Island, a favorite location for smugglers that jutted northward along the Rio

Grande at El Paso. About nine-thirty one morning a farmer and a policeman were inspecting the riverside when they were fired upon by two Mexicans who had crossed the international boundary line some two hundred yards away. The policeman returned the fire and the farmer ran to call for help. Two other officers came and searched the brush, but could not find the Mexican. They then notified Hamer, who drove to the scene with a friend and fellow officer, E. W. Walker. A short distance away they came upon the man and some twenty-five other smugglers, who had crossed the border in broad daylight to pick up a large cache of whiskey they had hidden on the American side of the border.

Although outnumbered, Hamer and Walker began to shoot it out with the smugglers. After some time the farmer returned with provost guards from the army base and El Paso policemen. The battle raged for some three hours, but a number of the smugglers managed to escape. Hamer's friend, Walker, was killed in the battle.[5]

A day or two later another group of bootleggers tried to run the blockade at the border by simply driving their car through at a high speed. Hamer and another federal agent hopped in a car and took out after them, chasing them right through the middle of El Paso. They finally got a clear field of fire and shot the tire of the bootleggers' car. It careened through a cemetery fence and overturned. The men inside were unhurt and tried to escape but were captured.[6] Early in 1921 Hamer was transferred to the Austin division of the prohibition service. Almost immediately he became embroiled in a situation that eventually made prohibition history. His boss in Austin was Chief Prohibition Officer in Texas and a man for whom Hamer had little respect. Hamer discovered that he was a member of a large bootlegging syndicate, known by the Runyanesque name of "The Black Hand."

As Chief Prohibition Officer, the man was able to protect the activities of the bootleggers as they filtered thousands of gallons of Mexican whiskey into the United States through Texas. The gang was Chicago-based and led by the toughest mobsters in the country.

Hamer was approached to join the syndicate, and for awhile played along, to collect evidence. Finally the Black Hand big shots became suspicious and ordered Hamer's boss to get rid of him.

On some pretext he had Hamer drive him out of town along a seldom-traveled dusty road and, as Hamer later recollected, seemed to be trying to muster the courage to kill Hamer. Sweat broke out on the man's face as Hamer stared coldly into his eyes, and finally the man whispered, "Let's go on back to town." Although able to sell out to the mobsters, he did not have the stomach to shoot a man looking him in the face.

When they got back to town, Hamer said, "Well, it's all up now. I've got enough evidence to put you away, and I guess I'd better do it before you get any other foolish notions."[7]

Hamer's boss surrendered and subsequently pled guilty in federal court to the charges of "conspiring to receive and conceal, transport and sell liquor brought into the United States from Mexico, in violation of prohibition laws."[8] Publicity given to the case went a long way toward curbing the activities of the notorious Black Hand, but for many years Hamer was a marked man, and several of the numerous attempts on his life were traced to the Chicago mobsters.

During the summer of 1921 Hamer was approached by Governor Pat Neff to accept a captaincy in the Texas Rangers. The governor was attempting to renew the quality of the Ranger service, but Hamer felt at first that it would be an impossible task. He finally accepted on September 21, 1921, after being offered the command of Company C, which was stationed at Del Rio.[9]

The loss of Hamer was a blow to the prohibition service. D. H. Morris wrote: "We regret losing Mr. Hamer very much, and I doubt there is a man in Texas so capable of filling the position that he held in Austin. Other men may be found, perhaps, as willing to work, and as conscientious, but Mr. Hamer's experience made him more than valuable."[10]

Hamer himself only commented that "I hate to leave Austin, but I sure will be glad to throw my leg over a horse again."[11]

When the Texas Rangers's youngest captain arrived at his command in Del Rio, he was in for a surprise. The laxity and incompetence that naturally resulted from the wholesale Ranger appointments was at its worst in the border company.

So Captain Hamer wired Austin that "things have been running mighty loose around here," and fired his entire company.[12]

12

"I'll kill anyone who tries to catch me."

The firing of Company C by its commander aroused exactly the attention Hamer desired at state headquarters. His company had not been given enough ammunition, blankets, or other supplies. There had been little or no coordination with higher headquarters, and neither the officials in Austin nor the Rangers at Del Rio seemed to have been doing much about border law enforcement.

Captain Hamer reenlisted those of his company in whom he had confidence and commented that he could do more good with these few than with twice the number of appointees that had been there when he arrived.[1] The authority and firmness with which he reorganized his company also enabled him to get the supplies that his men needed.

Hamer also renewed his friendships with Mexican rurales, and in a short time the southern Rio Grande was as peaceful as he had made it in 1919.

There was one large band of smugglers and outlaws, however, that had been operating out of Mexico for some time, under the leadership of a murderer named Ralph "Red" Lopez. The band smuggled drugs, bootlegged whiskey, rustled cattle, and robbed farmers and ranchers on both sides of the border.

Red Lopez had started his life as an outlaw after killing a man in Bingham, Utah, in 1913, while traveling in the United States as a rodeo performer. He had left behind a note to police officers: "Don't follow me. I'll kill anyone who tries to catch me."[2]

The affair developed into one of Utah's greatest manhunts. During the next year he blazed a trail that left some thirty known murders, from the Wasatch Mountains of Utah to the Texas border.

Lopez was an expert with a rifle and was one of the few gunmen who fired from the hip. One posse who chased him had six men out of thirty killed or wounded by Lopez's accuracy with a rifle.[3]

In 1914 Lopez and some bandits robbed a train along the border, killing nineteen of the twenty Americans that were passengers. This brought his total murders far beyond those of most of the outlaws of the older West.[4] He managed, nonetheless, to stay alive and to continue his banditry for nearly eight years.

Captain Hamer put Lopez as number one on his list of wanted men, and it was not long before he had some leads on the Lopez gang's activities. Acting on a tip from a Brownsville informer, Hamer and some of his company rode out along an irrigation ditch to the spot where they had been told Lopez would be arriving.

The tipster told Hamer to hide with his men in the irrigation ditch and said that he would meet Lopez at a point nearby. Hamer grew suspicious, however, after the informer left to get Lopez and moved his men across the ditch and behind a hump some yards away.

"I've got a feeling we've been led into a trap," he told the other Rangers.

Just before dark the Rangers watched twenty heavily armed Mexicans creep up behind the irrigation ditch. When they got to the point where the Rangers had been told to hide, they jumped up to open fire. From behind, Hamer stood up and shouted in Spanish, "Halt, We're officers of the law!"

Surprised, the Mexicans started firing. The first bullet creased Hamer's cheek, drawing blood. The Rangers returned the fire, and some thirty minutes later eleven of the bandits were dead and the rest had run away. Lopez was among the dead, killed by a bullet from Hamer's rifle. The bullet had pierced a gold watch in Lopez's top pocket, and the Rangers hung the watch in the Customs House in Laredo, where for many years it remained as a grisly reminder to border outlaws.[5] The State of Utah had offered a $3500.00 reward for Lopez, and Hamer split the reward with his Rangers.[6]

On January 1, 1922, Hamer was transferred to Ranger headquarters in Austin, where the governor made him Headquarters Company captain. From this position, as senior captain of all the Texas Rangers, Hamer sent Rangers to trouble spots and, in almost every instance, assigned himself to the most difficult and dangerous cases. As Webb succinctly put it, "he saw service in all parts of the state, while his reputation continued to grow."[7]

The move to Austin marked the end of Hamer's horseback days as a Ranger. When he settled down in Austin, Hamer started wearing shoes and a business suit.

"Boots were made for riding," he commented, "and I've got no desire to look like a 'pharmaceutical' Ranger." He had nothing but disgust for the "drugstore cowboy" types who sported knee-high boots, ten-gallon hats, and fancy cowboy apparel.

Governor Pat Neff considered the revitalization of the Ranger force under Hamer as one of the most important events in his administration. He later wrote: "During my four years as Governor, the Rangers were in constant use. They were called upon on an average of once a month during my administration to protect prisoners who were being tried, and to prevent mob violence. Almost every day demands of some kind were made for them. We could not begin to respond to all calls. In addition, we sent them to places without any request from anyone, and without the knowledge generally. Wherever they did go, they went quietly to begin their investigations. We never thought it wise to give to the press what the Rangers were doing. We sometimes read editorials criticizing the Governor for not sending the Rangers to a certain point, when in reality, as secret service men, they had been there for days. The mere presence of a Texas Ranger creates regard for law. . . . The Rangers, during my administration, were in every way worthy of the ideals, the traditions, and the devotion to duty that characterized their predecessors."[8]

Hamer's reputation had preceded him to Austin, as evidenced by this newspaper editorial about one of his first encounters:

"George gave a roadside party out in the brush country several miles from Austin. They were having a good time, until a fellow by the name of Frank Hamer came up. He seemed to be connected with the rangers, in some way. George didn't know Frank very well and he threatened to use his influence on the job that Frank was holding. Somehow the threats didn't scare the intruder, he looked like a man that was hard to scare, so the resourceful George tacked to the wind, he bethought himself of his purse. He hated to part with the money but he would do it to clear up an embarrassing situation. He offered to toss the man Frank Hamer a few plunks and let it go at that, but a few plunks didn't seem to interest the officer, he then raised his ante to one thousand plunks, and the officer made him shut up, they say he does that way sometimes."

"'George shut up!' They say he snapped his mouth together so hard he loosened three molars and one bicuspid. After awhile George was booked and out on bond, and the man Frank Hamer departed for other duties."

Hamer's first major task as headquarters captain was the cleaning up of Mexia, an oil boomtown located seventy miles southeast of Dallas. Until 1921 Mexia was a quiet country town of 2,500 inhabitants, but during the fall of that year oil was discovered in the vicinity. Almost overnight some 30,000 people rushed to the town, seeking fortunes not only in oil but in those numerous ways that grafters, gamblers, speculators, and outright criminals manage to grab hold of any place where easy wealth and loose money abound.

The narrow, muddy streets were choked with vagrants. The local hotel was turned into a public gambling house, with two open crap tables, continuous poker games, and open bars selling bootleg liquor. Undefied by the local law officers, the newcomers started eighteen other wide-open gambling halls, some in tents thrown up in the main business district. Stills were set up in the surrounding woods, and within a few weeks Mexia was one of the most corrupt and lawless cities Texas had ever seen.

The older citizens complained to Governor Neff, who took up the matter with Captain Hamer and Adjutant General Thomas D. Barton. They arranged for several undercover agents to slip into the area and report on the underworld activities in Mexia. The agents reported, according to General Jacob F. Wolters, that "within four miles of the city of Mexia, in Freestone County . . . there was constructed an elaborate building called the 'Winter Garden.' A large sign was erected on the road with the words 'Winter Garden' painted thereon in large letters. . . . Within this Winter Garden was operated a public gambling establishment, viz., a roulette wheel, chuck-a-luck, blackjack, crap tables, poker tables, and various other gambling games. There was . . . a bar from which red liquor and white corn liquor was dispensed. These liquors were served not only from the bar, but at tables in the cafe. An armed guard was maintained on the road leading from the public highway to the Winter Garden."[10]

Patrons were frisked and led into the gambling hall, where pistol-packing bouncers made a more thorough search of each visitor. Behind the latticework overlooking the main hall, guards were placed with shotguns, machine guns, and rifles. "This place," the report stated, "was openly conducted in defiance of the law . . . [and] was visited by thousands of people, including County Peace Officers from Limestone and Freestone Counties."[11]

A deputy sheriff from Freestone County, the report continued, sold gamblers four acres of county land in sight of the highway, on which "was constructed a building similar to the Winter Garden called the 'Chicken Farm.' Here open gambling . . . and whiskey selling were conducted. The same system of armed guards was maintained at the Chicken Farm."[12] More advanced than the Winter Garden, the Chicken Farm boasted tall watchtowers similar to those used on prison farms, as well as trap doors inside the gambling hall through which patrons could flee if raided.

The report disturbed Governor Neff more than anything else during his whole administration. He immediately dispatched Hamer and a company of Rangers to clean up the town. On January 7, 1922, Hamer and his men, along with Tom Hickman, General Barton himself, and two federal officers—a total of twenty-two men—set out for Mexia. Hamer and half the men raided the Winter Garden, whereas Hickman and the others hit the Chicken Farm. With commando-like efficiency both squads shot their way into the establishments and captured most of the owners and their henchmen. Besides the gambling equipment, more than 660 quarts of whiskey, a large horde of narcotics, and a virtual arsenal of weapons were captured.[13] Making use of the elaborate protective systems, Hamer set up headquarters in the Winter Garden for operations against the town itself.

Bert Griffith writes that "twenty percent of Mexia's population was in jail or under bail within 72 hours after the Rangers rode into town." Exaggerated as that statement might be, it is true that Hamer was arresting criminals faster than he was able to dispose of them. Hamer called the governor, told him he needed help to guard the prisoners, and explained that he was severely hampered by the necessity of obtaining search warrants. Because many Mexia officials were crooked, his targets were being tipped off as soon as he obtained the search warrants by the issuing officials. After a brief conference, Governor Neff declared martial law on February 2, 1922.[14]

Texas National Guardsmen arrived the next day and turned the Winter Garden into a prison camp. Major Chester H. Machen set up a military court to examine the prisoners. The Rangers, freed by the martial law, were able to raid gamblers, dope peddlers, and stills, and they arrested a large number of town and county officials who were charged, and later convicted, of either aiding or actually participating in the illicit activities.

"So scarce did liquor become in Mexia," General Wolters reported, "that during the last week of our stay habitual drunkards were arrested and found in possession of bottles of denatured alcohol labeled in red print 'POISONOUS' with the warning that internal use will result in blindness, paralysis, and death."[15]

A total of 602 arrests were made, more than 3000 undesirables run out of town, 27 stills captured with 9,080 quarts of bootleg whiskey, 53 stolen automobiles recovered, a nationwide narcotics ring broken up, and the largest amount of gambling equipment ever recovered up to that time destroyed. From more than a thousand witnesses the Rangers learned that many local officials were taking payoffs of up to $250 per day and that out-of-state crime syndicates were behind most of the illegal activities.[16]

Martial law was lifted and Hamer returned to Austin. Governor Neff wrote to Hamer on March 6: "I desire to express to you my appreciation of the effective service which you [in Mexia]. . . . The bearing and conduct of the individual members of the entire organization was in every way consistent with the ideals of our Ranger service, and I have heard from the citizens of Mexia and the surrounding community, many words of commendation for the accomplishments and demeanor of the Texas Rangers. I am sure that your personal contributions to this well-earned commendation will always be a pleasant recollection to you."[17]

General Wolters wrote: "It would be difficult to find in this or any other state two more efficient officers than [Hamer and Hickman], both possessing the combination of intelligence, physical strength, power of endurance, and energy. They are fully equipped to cope with the lawless element at all times and under all circumstances."[18]

13
"Is it Santa Claus?"

During the last days of the occupation of Mexia, the Rangers destroyed most of the captured gambling and bootlegging equipment. Hamer was asked to exhibit his renowned shooting ability. Some of the soldiers threw confiscated three-inch butter dishes in the air while Hamer shot them with his .25-caliber Remington autoloading rifle. An agent of Remington Arms had heard that the Ranger captain would be shooting and drove out from Dallas to watch. He took motion pictures of Hamer as he shot more than a hundred consecutive dishes out of the air. He sent the film to his parent company. The Remington people were so impressed, not only with the marksmanship, but also with Hamer's previous exploits and adventures, that they had a special .30-caliber model 8F autoloading rifle made for the captain. The rifle was heavily engraved with scenes from his career and had his name and the Texas seal inlayed in gold. Unbeknownst to Hamer, the company sent this fine presentation piece to Petmecky's sporting goods store in Austin. Petmecky called Hamer on the package's arrival, and the Ranger captain was greatly pleased and surprised on seeing the gun. The rifle became Hamer's favorite deer rifle, and later tales of his fantastic marksmanship with it became legendary.[1]

Hamer's favorite pistol was "Old Lucky," a "C"-engraved, .45-caliber Colt single-action revolver, and he was even better with it than a rifle. Captain Hamer was once challenged to a pistol contest by a sheriff who had a reputation as a crack shot. While the targets were being set up, states Kinney, "Hamer announced he was going to hit a small, glittering rock more than a hundred yards away.

Using his left hand as he always did he elevated the muzzle of his .45 to the firing angle of a heavy artillery piece—his first shot kicked the stone into the air. His competitor kept his pistol holstered.

"I said a pistol match," the sheriff grumbled. "Forty yard limits. Anything over that is rifle distance.'"[2]

Incidents like this made Hamer one of the most famous shots in the Southwest, but it remained for historian Webb to put the capper on Hamer's shooting powers "Hamer," said Webb in 1935, "has spent much time on the rifle ranges, and on one occasion when the target was too far to see where the bullets hit, he sat by the rifleman and called the shots *before they hit.* He can see the bullet, which looks like a bee, enveloped in a tiny cloud of heat waves produced by friction between lead and air. The discharge from a shotgun 'looks like a swarm of gnats.'"[3]

Webb, not one to report by rumor, found that Hamer's abilities had been discussed in a contemporary "treatise on ballistics," and were true in every detail.[4]

Hamer was also sent by the governor into the notorious Ganders Slough extension of the Luling oil field. Luling, in southern Caldwell County, joined the growing list of oil boom towns of the early twenties during the summer of 1922, and the Ganders Slough extension in neighboring Guadalupe County became a center of vice and corruption.

Captain Hamer led a small raiding party consisting of W. E. Mayberry, Harry Nolan, and Lee Shannon into the area, despite telephone and written threats against his life. As usual, they broke the crime organization completely, capturing stills and gambling equipment and also arresting a local peace officer for dereliction of duty.[5] In the fall of 1922 the San Saba Baptist Church in San Saba was burned to the ground after the church's pastor gave a sermon defending prohibition. Hamer found clues at the scene and followed two suspects to a downtown Austin hotel. He walked in on the men while they were planning another arson and arrested both without incident.[6]

A vicious political feud erupted in the coastal town of Corpus Christi in 1922. A political machine had been in control of city and county politics for a long time, and was in serious danger of being turned out in the next election. The citizenry had so strongly turned against the machine that there was no hope of winning the election even by ballot-stuffing—a favorite trick in South Texas. The organization, therefore, set about to intimidate the opposition so badly that opposing candidates would withdraw.

G. E. Warren, a leader of the new opposition, was a local grocer. In June 1922 the sheriff of the county strode into Warren's small store on Railroad Avenue and went up to the counter. Uttering strong curses, and in front of several customers and Warren's wife, the sheriff leaned across the counter, grabbed Warren by the collar, and began to work him over. Mrs. Warren ran to a telephone in the back of the store and called a neighbor, Fred Roberts, to come to her husband's aid. By this time the sheriff had walked outside the store, having left the bleeding Warren on the floor.

Roberts went in through the back door, helped Mrs. Warren treat her wounded husband, and went back out the door to his car. As he did so the sheriff walked up to him, said a few words, then pulled out his pistol and fired a full clip of shells into his body from a few feet away. Roberts died instantly.

Meanwhile, the deputy sheriff and a constable ran up the window in front of Warren's store and began to fire into the store itself.

Mrs. Warren and the other customers dropped to the floor as glass shattered over them and bullets ricocheted through the small store. The sheriff, deputy, and constable then departed. No attempt was made to arrest them, although warrants were made out.[7]

The citizens, greatly incensed, applied to the governor. The governor sent Hamer and some of his Rangers to investigate.

When Captain Hamer arrived in Corpus Christi, he learned that the murderers were barricaded inside the county courthouse, with thirty or forty henchmen armed with shotguns and rifles. Hamer told the other Rangers to stand back, and approached the armed crowd alone. They stood aside and he marched into the courthouse. He kicked open the large double doors of the courtroom and found himself standing in front of a dozen men who were pointing rifles, shotguns, and pistols at him.

"I'm Frank Hamer, Texas Ranger," he said, with an icy stare. "I have a warrant for the arrest of the men involved in the murder of Fred Roberts. The rest of you put up those guns and get the hell out of here."

He walked up to the accused men and began to read the warrants. As he did so, the others—overpowered by the strength of Hamer's personality alone—slowly began to file out of the courtroom. Hamer, his handcuffed prisoners, and the other Rangers departed for the county jailhouse. The Rangers stayed in Corpus Christi until after the elections, and then departed for Austin.[8]

A Corpus Christi newspaper editorialized: "They came near dying when Captain Frank Hamer of Austin showed up on the scene. . . . Hamer is the man they all dreaded, and when he got here they all got good and remained so as long as he was on the job. This is all that saved the day . . . as well as prevented a wholesale killing which was so imminent that it did not look inviting. But they took to the tall timber when the Rangers made their appearance."[9]

The grateful citizenry of Corpus Christi presented Captain Hamer with a silver-plated .45-caliber Colt single-action revolver, inscribed: "Capt. Frank Hamer, State Ranger, presented by the citizens of Corpus Christi, 7-22-22."[10]

After two eventful years Hamer took a long-needed Christmas vacation with his family. They had settled on Riverside Drive in Austin in a comfortable home atop a hill overlooking the city, a home in which they would live for more than thirty years.

On Christmas Eve, Hamer sat with his family by the Christmas tree, engaging in small talk while decorating the tree. Young Beverly, his stepdaughter, was out on a date. Shortly after eleven a knock was heard at the door. Laughing, thinking it was her daughter and date, Gladys went to the door, opened it wide, and said, "Boo!"

She spoke right into the stomach of a tall young man she had never seen before. Both were shocked, and after a few silent moments the man said, "I want Hamer."

Still smiling, Gladys called her husband, who came to the door. "I'm Frank Hamer," he said, extending his hand.

The man did not respond, and only mumbled that he wanted to see Hamer outside. Finally, he whipped out a pistol and started to shoot Hamer. The captain, still standing casually in the doorway, slapped the man hard with his left hand. The blow knocked the man off the porch and the steep front steps.

Gladys rushed to the door with Hamer's pistol, but the man had never stopped from his tumble down the steps and was running down the street. Hamer refused the pistol, but picked up a milk bottle to throw at the man. Hamer changed his mind, though, and the lawman and his wife watched the man disappear around a corner.

Young Billy Hamer was awakened and came running downstairs shouting, "Is it Santa Claus? Is it Santa Claus?"[11]

The remarkable Hamers then returned to their Christmas decorating. Hamer always laughed the incident off, particularly when on the next morning they found the murderer's pistol, a nickel-plated, nine-shot automatic that was more of a collector's item than a murder weapon. The captain never reported the assassination attempt to the police, commenting: "There's no need to. With that kind of man you just let him run out enough rope and he'll hang himself."[12]

Although Hamer never told whether the assassin represented the Mexia mobsters, the Corpus Christi bombers, the underworld bootleg syndicate, a former gubernatorial administration, or someone wanting to settle an even older score, the man never came back to try Hamer again and was soon killed in a car accident.[13]

14

"'Capt. Hamer' was the nicest crook I ever met."

In 1925 the Fergusons came back into power in Texas. Former Governor Jim Ferguson, unable to run for office himself as a result of his impeachment, put his wife, Miriam, up for the office. When she won the election, she became the first female governor in American history, but the reins of government were firmly in control of the man of the family. A few days after the inaugural, Hamer resigned from the Ranger service.

The Austin *Statesman* reported: "Resignation of Capt. Frank Hamer, Dean of the Texas Rangers and oldest man in point of service was accepted here late today by Adjutant General Mark McGee. . . . With the resignation, Capt. Hamer, one of the most spectacular peace officers in Texas passes from the Ranger Service. Capt. Hamer has figured in many of the greatest battles against law breakers in Texas, since he first entered the service in 1907."[1]

Many Texas citizens were as upset as Hamer about the new administration leaders. Among these was ex-Governor Neff, who wrote Hamer: "I regret very much your resignation for the reason that I know full well the valuable, faithful, and efficient services you have rendered for so many years to the State. I want you to know that during the four years of my administration I appreciated and still appreciate the services rendered by you in behalf of law and order. When you went anywhere any time in the name of the State to uphold the law and maintain peace, I never lost any sleep, because I knew the work would be done just as it should be."[2]

So great was the public feeling against Hamer's resignation that even the Fergusons appealed to Hamer to return. After some time Hamer relented, when he was assured that the wholesale drugstore-cowboy appointments to the Ranger service of the former Ferguson administrations would not occur again.

Hamer's hardest days as a peace officer followed. Working under an administration in which he had no confidence, he pursued the task of keeping the peace virtually without support, and his Rangers stood out as never before as the finest law enforcement body in the world.

In November 1925, Hamer and W. W. Taylor went down to Del Rio to investigate a case, and joined Hamer's brother Harrison, who was customs agent there. The three men went out one night to a certain spot along the border, hoping to catch some smugglers in the act.[3] As they brought their car to a halt, they were met with a barrage of fire from across the river. The three men quickly took cover and a heated battle blazed for a few moments, whereupon their assailants—those left alive—fled for a safer ground. The Del Rio newspaper commented the next morning:

"Those Mexicans who fired on Frank Hamer just didn't know what they were doing. Good thing they were across the river border, for to even think of pointing a gun at Hamer in Texas means disaster."[4]

During 1925, trouble broke out among Texas cattlemen over, of all things, cattle ticks. Known as the "Tick War," this brief episode occurred when tick fever among Texas cattle brought on quarantines in some areas and general cattle dipping regulations for the entire Texas cattle industry. The latter, a mandatory dipping law, was one of the first strenuous government regulations concerning cattlemen since the fencing laws of a few decades before.

Most cattlemen, by this time, had adjusted themselves to the idea of state regulations, and most realized the general value to everyone concerned of the activities of the Livestock Sanitary Commission. But there were, as always, a few old-timers who defied the law.

Right in the center of the fever tick belt stood the Damon Ranch, just west of the Colorado River in Wharton County. When the tick inspectors approached Forrest Damon to dip his cattle, the grizzled bachelor refused, and threatened to shoot anyone who tried to touch his cattle. The inspectors went to Governor Dan Moody, and Governor Moody called on Hamer.

Diplomacy was always Hamer's short suit. He knew that old man Damon a short time previously had managed to keep a state highway from crossing his range by threatening to shoot the road workers. Hamer felt no good would come from a lot of talk. He went directly to the rancher and said, "Damon, the law says that you've got to let your cattle be dipped, by damn, and that's exactly what you're going to do."

"I don't give a damn what the law says," replied the stubborn cattleman. "These are my cattle and I'll kill any man who lays a hand on them without my permission."

"All right, Damon," Hamer stated, "if that's the way you want it, I'll give you two weeks to get your cattle dipped, then I'll be back."[5] Damon was so enraged at being told to dip his cattle that he publicly declared he would kill Hamer and any inspectors who set foot on his property. He charged Hamer with illegal entry, but the charge failed to hold up because Hamer had been acting on the governor's orders. Hamer knew the old man was just being ornery but also realized he might have to kill Damon if he went back and Damon started shooting at him. So he arranged for W. W. Sterling and W. R. Smith to go see Damon, taking the inspectors with them. Sterling later described the encounter:

"Accompanied by Ranger W. R. Smith, I left our station in Falfurrias at two o'clock in the morning and six hours later we arrived at the dipping vat. It was in the woods about a mile from the ranch house, and several cars of inspectors were waiting for us. They had placed their automobiles in the form of a hollow square, it looked like they were better prepared to repel invaders than to dip cattle. I left Bob Smith at the vat, and told them to go ahead with their work. The chief inspector said, 'No, sir, we are not going to do a thing until you have Damon in custody.'"

"Instructing Smith that if I did not return in half an hour to proceed with the dipping, I drove to the ranch house and stopped at the front gate. Damon was standing in the doorway. His great bulk filled it so completely that I could not see his hands. I got out of my open car, called a pleasant good morning to him, and started walking toward the gallery. He had a small arsenal in the house, with shot gun, pistol and Winchester within easy reach. I wore a short brush jacket and my holstered six-shooter was in plain sight. I did not give any indication that the situation called for gun play.

"The absence of rough talk or drawn pistol disconcerted and puzzled him. It was not the approach he had anticipated. I stated my name and business. Damon growled, 'You're the gun man the governor sent down here to kill me, ain't you?'"

"No," I replied, "I'm not here to kill you. We're only going to dip your cattle."

"You can't dip them," he blurted out.

"We're already dipping them," I informed him. "Sit down and be quiet and we'll get along fine."

"He stared at me in amazement. We went into the room that served as his office and sleeping quarters."

"'Mr. Damon, you appear to be a good citizen,'" I said. "Why did you bow your neck against tick eradication?'"

"'Well, for one thing," he replied, I don't like to be MADE to do anything. . . . Those ticks you are killing belong to me. I pay taxes on them and they are mine. I can do as I please with them.'"

"I was astounded by this weird argument but finally managed to say, 'Suppose you had smallpox. They would also belong to you, but you would not be permitted to scatter them all over the country, would you?'

"This seemed to register with him, and nothing more was said about dipping."

"Forrest Damon and I became good friends after the tick episode. He told me frankly that he had made up his mind to shoot it out with the next man who attempted to dip his cattle, even though he might be a Ranger. The old-timer believed that his rights had been violated. He was all riled up after the encounter with Capt. Hamer."[6]

For several months late in 1925 a small, talkative fellow traveled up and down the Pacific Coast posing as "Capt. Frank A. Hamer of the Texas Rangers." He introduced himself at the American Legion Convention in Portland, Oregon, using Hamer's name and posing as a 32nd Degree Mason and claiming to have fought with Roosevelt in Cuba, with General Funstrum in the Philippines, finally becoming a Texas Ranger. He said that he had killed more than 250 Mexicans along the border. He claimed to have chased one fugitive all the way to Cape Town, South Africa, at an expense to the State of Texas of more than nine thousand dollars, only to have Governor "Ma" Ferguson pardon the man as soon as he brought him in.

With nothing more than this pitch as his credentials, the man was able to go from convention to convention using Hamer's name and passing hot checks all along the way. At times he used the name "Capt. Buck Miller," and several other aliases. When Hamer got word, he wrote several newspapers in California and Oregon.

The Portland *Oregonian* carried a front-page article February 2, 1926, headed "BREEZY 'RANGER' SOUGHT AS FAKER, TEXAS OUTFIT DISOWNS TALKATIVE CALLER." The story read, in part: "[The imposter] played a two or three day engagement in Portland at the Venson Hotel and then disappeared. He induced a number of the members of the Portland Shrine to cash checks for him. He went by the name of Capt. Frank A. Hamer of Del Rio, of the Rangers, and now the real Capt. Hamer writes that the fellow is an imposter, a swindler, and a few other things and that he has no connection with the historic Texas Ranger captain. . . . The real Capt. Hamer advises that the police, hotel, and Shrine bodies along the Pacific coast be notified immediately to look out for the 'hero.'"[7] With the heat on, out West the spurtous Ranger headed toward Texas. On July 15, 1926, he went to the headquarters of a political candidate in San Antonio, still posing as Hamer, and offered to contribute a hundred dollars to the man's campaign. He gave the campaign manager a check on a Houston bank for $350.00, arranged with the manager to have it cashed, contributed the $100.00, and pocketed the $250.00 change. In the next few days he bought clothes, hats, food, and a number of other items, always using Hamer's name and cashing checks as often as possible.

Then, with unfathomable gall, he went to Austin. Going to the office of the Railway Express, he told the agent that he wanted to purchase a thousand dollars worth of traveler's checks, identifying himself as Hamer. The agent in charge, E. I. Bodell, was acquainted with Hamer and was taken aback at the sight of the short, mustachioed man. He told him to call back the next morning for the checks and as soon as the man had left he called the police.

R. D. "Boss" Thorp of the Austin police called Hamer and the two set out after the man, who never returned to the express agency. The man appeared in New Orleans, then Dallas, and went back to San Antonio. Hamer notified local authorities, who arrested him in front of the Russell Building in San Antonio. Hamer and Thorp picked the imposter up and brought him to Austin. His fingerprints identified the man as John B. Sawyer, wanted since 1909 for pick-pocketing, larceny, check forging, impersonation, and escape from the Texas State Penitentiary. Confronted with his record, Sawyer confessed that he had escaped on March 3, 1925, and since that time had been traveling under the name "Captain Frank Hamer" and had used the name to forge checks in Texas, Louisiana, Mississippi, South Carolina, Florida, Colorado, California, Virginia, Pennsylvania, Georgia, Maryland, New Jersey, New York, Michigan, Illinois, Missouri, Oregon, Alabama, Tennessee, West Virginia, Rhode Island, Connecticut, and in Winnipeg and Vancouver, Canada. He was convicted and sent to a federal prison.[8]

Among his fellow Rangers, Hamer never lived it down. They photographed Hamer and Sawyer together, Hamer towering nearly a foot taller and a hundred pounds heavier. The other Rangers, however, swore that the two must be twins, and that their personalities were just alike. Hamer took all the kidding in stride, and even made friends with the imposter while he was being held in Austin. "'Capt. Hamer' was the nicest crook I ever met," Hamer always said.[9]

15

"I've never been as scared as I was when Frank's big hand landed on my shoulder."

Even when he was headquarters captain, Hamer always handled the most difficult cases himself. He would disappear for days—or even weeks—at a time. Then, one afternoon, he would walk back into his office with the case wrapped up. The governors and adjutant generals that he served under learned to anticipate his actions. When he was hard at work on a case, most of the everyday paper work was shuffled to other desks. Consequently, Hamer's reports on file at Ranger headquarters were almost nonexistent. More verbose Rangers of the period left voluminous files with detailed, sometimes even hour-by-hour, reports of their activities. If filed at all, Captain Hamer's included no more than three or four lines.

Even while working alone on a case, Hamer proved to be one of the greatest sleuths of his time. Automobile thefts reached a nationwide high early in 1927, and Hamer learned that one of the largest theft rings in the nation centered in Texas. He ordered the Rangers out to investigate. They reported that the theft ring was active, but no one could locate them. Hamer called in his men and set out alone.

After several days of investigation, he learned that the ring was operating in Llano County. More silent investigation pinned down the leaders of the gang. By the end of the week, Hamer was ready to make his arrests. His plans, however, included more than rounding up the gang leaders. Scores of car dealers and other individuals had obtained cars without proper title, knowing full well that the cars were stolen. Hamer knew that there was little chance of returning these cars to their rightful owners because the car dealers would lose their money.

Hamer pondered the problem over a bowl of chili in a small, greasy cafe in Llano. When he pulled a telegram pertaining to another matter from his pocket, he overheard one of the waitresses whisper to another, "I'd give ten bucks to know what that telegram's about!"

Hamer left the cafe, made a few inquiries, and learned that the waitress was the sweetheart of one of the gang's ringleaders. At the local telegraph office, Hamer picked up a telegram blank and wrote:

"To Capt. Frank A. Hamer, Llano, Texas

"Do not prosecute innocent purchasers who turn in cars. Arrest all others for complicity and hold in jail for criminal prosecution. (signed) Aldrich, Adjutant-General."

Hamer crumpled the spurious telegram and stuck it haphazardly in his hip pocket. That evening he returned to the cafe and ordered another bowl of chili. When he had finished, he pulled out his handkerchief to blow his nose, letting the telegram fall to the floor. Pretending not to notice, he left the cafe. Out of the corner of his eye, he saw the waitress "land on that telegram like a duck on a June bug."[1]

Early the next morning a man knocked on Hamer's hotel room door.

"Well?" Hamer answered.

"I understand you're looking for some stolen cars out here," Hamer's caller said.

"Yes, I am," Hamer replied.

"Well, I think the car I bought several weeks ago was stolen," the man continued, "and I'd like to turn it over to you."

"Well, come on in and I'll give you a receipt," Frank replied. Soon after the "innocent purchaser" left Hamer's room, more and more people came to Hamer to turn in their stolen automobiles. By the end of the day more than fifty automobiles had been recovered. As Hamer guessed, the waitress had spread the news all over town. Not only did the buyers turn in their cars, but the thieves, hoping to avoid prosecution, did so also. Captain Hamer's ingenuity broke the entire ring of hijackers, as well as recovering the stolen automobiles of more than fifty citizens.[2]

Not long after the Llano incident, Hamer entered an Austin speak-easy searching for the leader of a large ring of bootleggers. Bill Kuykendall, one of Hamer's close friends and a prominent Texas rancher, was taking his ease in the place.

"I was sitting at the bar having a drink," Kuykendall recalls, "when I felt a hand on my shoulder. I turned around and nearly swallowed my tongue in fright. There standing over me was Frank Hamer! I didn't know what to do, so I just sat there looking like a damn fool."

"Hello, Bill, How's everything?"

"What in hell are you doing here?"

"Oh, just nosing around,' Frank replied, sitting down next to me. By this time, I had recovered from my initial shock. After watching the crowd for a few minutes, Frank left. He was after much bigger game that night and had neither the time nor the inclination for hauling in local citizens."

"I've lived through some tough spots in my life—both at home and during the war," Kuykendall recalls, "but I've never been quite so scared as when Frank's big hand landed on my shoulder!"[3]

The famed humorist Will Rogers made a visit to Austin during the 1920s. He attended a dinner with the Governors Ferguson, but left early, according to the newspapers, "having expressed a desire to 'chat awhile' with Frank Hamer, best known of the Texas Rangers."[4] Rogers was given the title "Honorary Ranger," and visited Austin several times in later years to see Hamer, W. W. Sterling, and other Rangers. The real Texas Rangers always had a particular fascination for visiting movie stars and celebrities from outside Texas.

During the 1920s and early 1930s, the noted historian, Webb, was researching his book on the Texas Rangers. He and Hamer became acquainted, and Hamer lent Webb a helping hand whenever he could. In 1927, while investigating a case near Round Rock, Texas, Hamer discovered that one of the outlaws who had ridden with Sam Bass was still alive. The outlaw had been with Bass when he was killed near Round Rock in a bloody battle with Texas Rangers on July 19, 1878. He had managed to escape and had never been heard from since.

Following up a few clues, Hamer learned that the old outlaw, Frank Jackson, was now seventy-eight years old and living peacefully in New Mexico. Hamer knew that Webb would want to interview the retired renegade, and the two men tried to correspond with Jackson. However, the old man "disappeared," afraid that he might be brought to trial for crimes he had committed more than fifty years before. Hamer and Webb checked with the adjutant general and learned that Jackson would not be brought to trial for deeds committed nearly a half century earlier and that he was perfectly free to return to his old home in Texas to live out his remaining days.

Webb and Hamer wrote to author Eugene Manlove Rhodes and enlisted his aid. On June 13, 1927, Rhodes wrote from Santa Fe that they might get Jackson's friend, Jim Hinkle, former governor of New Mexico to intercede. "Hinkle's association with the matter," Rhodes wrote, "will be to Jackson another guarantee of good faith. . . . It isn't going to be easy to convince Jackson."[5]

But Jackson, who had managed to hide out successfully for so many decades, was not about to take the word of a Texas Ranger.

Webb and Hamer obtained a letter from the governor, stating that Jackson could return to Texas without fear of arrest. Jackson, nonetheless, remained unconvinced.[6] Webb wrote Hamer from Dallas, "We ought to go pretty slow, because if we get this old bird into trouble, we'll have to get him out. They can't prove anything on him, but they can deal him some misery if they get mean and lawyer-like enough."[7] Webb and Hamer were still trying to get Jackson to return, when the old gunslinger died. Webb had lost a valuable interview that would have added considerable knowledge about the saga of Bass and the Texas Rangers.

Webb and Hamer formed a close friendship. Webb often sat in on Hamer's poker club, mostly made up of other Rangers. "Poker," said Webb, "was Hamer's most serious fault." He wrote:

"The poker club meets about once a week in his dining-room, and the game is played in the presence of his family, but not a penny changes hands. The poker chips are the best that money can buy, the kind that are used in professional gambling houses. They bear the initials of a wealthy Texan who undertook to run a gambling house near Houston and did so until Captain Hamer raided the house, broke up the equipment, and kept the chips as souvenirs."

"These poker games show Frank Hamer at his worst. He has been known to practice deception by acting as if he held four aces when in reality he held nothing more than two deuces. Quite often he acts with such convincingness as to steal practically everything on the table, but he claims that he was taught by that great mentor, Captain J. B. Wheatley, who, it must be said, continues occasionally to teach him something. Both of these men have spent many years in reading the human countenance and detecting the truth behind all that hides it, and they persist in carrying this training to the dining room table with terrible results for their opponents. The legislature should investigate them and pass a law of restraint. It would meet the hearty approval of such members as Best, Gault, Green, Smith, and—others."[8]

Home and blacksmith shop at Oxford, Texas, near Llano, where Hamer grew up.

Duke Hudson, left, and Frank Hamer, right, on a visit to
Portales, New Mexico, before the turn of the century.

Frank Hamer, cowboy, about 1903.

Duke Hudson and Frank Hamer in their wrangler days.

Sheffield, Texas, about 1906, where Hamer first joined the Texas Rangers.

Captain John H. Rogers, Hamer's first captain in the Texas Rangers.

"I'M FRANK HAMER"

ENLISTMENT, OATH OF SERVICE, AND DESCRIPTION RANGER FORCE.

Company __C__ Ranger Force, Station __Alpine Texas__

THE STATE OF TEXAS,
COUNTY OF __Pecos__

I, __Frances Augustus Hamer__ , born in __1884__ in the State of __Texas__ , aged __22__ years and __1__ months, and by occupation a __Cow Boy__ do hereby acknowledge to have voluntarily enlisted this day of __21 April__ , 190 __6__ , as a private in the Ranger Force of this State, for the period of two years, unless sooner discharged by proper authority. And I do also agree to accept from the State of Texas such bounty, pay, subsistence and other expenses as are or may be established by law. And I do solemnly swear that I will faithfully and impartially discharge and perform all the duties incumbent on me as an officer of the Ranger Force according to the best of my skill and ability, agreeably to the Constitution and laws of the United States and of this State, and I do further solemnly swear that since the adoption of the Constitution of this State, I being a citizen of this State, have not fought a duel with deadly weapons, nor have I acted as second in carrying a challenge, or aided, advised or assisted any person thus offending. And I furthermore swear that I have not, directly nor indirectly, paid, offered or promised to pay, contributed nor promised to contribute, any money or valuable thing, or promised any public office or employment, to secure my appointment. So help me God.   __F. A. Hamer.__

Subscribed and sworn to before me this __21__ day of __April__ A. D. 190 __6__
__J. B. Hardspeth justice of Peace and
Ex Officio notary public for Pecos County
Texas__

I certify that __F. A. Hamer__ , the above named man, has been carefully examined by me previous to his enlistment and to the best of my knowledge and belief he is physically able, competent to and will faithfully perform the duties incumbent on him in accordance with law. This man is __22__ years __Blue__ months of age. Height __6__ feet __3__ inches. Complexion __Light__ Eyes __
Hair __Brown__ Born at __Fairview__ County of __Wilson__ State of __Texas__
Occupation __Cow Boy__ Married or single __Single__ Previous service __None__

Remarks _____

__J. H. Rogers__
Captain Co. "C" Ranger Force.

Frank Hamer enters the Texas Rangers under Capt. John H. Rogers, Sheffield, Texas, April 21, 1906

Frank Hamer enters the Texas Rangers under Capt. John H. Rogers, Sheffield, Texas, April 26, 2006.

Hamer and Duke Hudson.

Hamer and his Ranger company, about 1907. Hamer is in the center row, second from left.

Hamer, in black hat, with other Rangers in
Del Rio.

Frank Hamer, the day after killing Ed Putnam.

Captain W. W. Taylor of the Texas Rangers.

Hamer as Marchal of Navasota.

Marshal Hamer, far left, leading a parade in Navasota, 1909.

Hamer and Cal Phelps having some fun near Alpine, Texas.

Frank Hamer and Bugler.

Captain Hamer on Bugler.

Captain Charles Stevens, center, and Captain Hamer, right, hold a parley with Mexican rurales near Tomate Bend.

Captain Charles Stevens and a Mexican rurale leader agree on plans for catching bandits along the border.

Frank Hamer in action.

Hamer, in black hat, crossing the Rio Grande.

Mexican rurales.

Harrison Hamer, brother of Frank Hamer.

Frank Hamer on his trip to California, 1918.

The Reel Thing and the Real Thing; Tom Mix and Frank Hamer.

Frank Hamer and some friends.

Dead Mexican bandits near Brownsville. *John H. Jenkins Collection.*

Dead Mexican bandits. *John H. Jenkins Collection.*

Mexican revolutionaries.

Mexican revolutionaries at battle from the top of a hill just south of the Rio Grande.

Frank Hamer's Identity Card, Brownsville, 1919.

Captain Hamer and M. T. Gonzales in El Paso.

Frank Hamer about 1921.

Texas Rangers on the state capitol grounds, 1920. Hamer is in the middle row, fourth from left.

General Jacob F. Wolters at Mexia.

Texas Rangers on the steps of the state capitol. Adjutant General Thomas D. Barton is center front, with Hamer to his left.

Hamer and his men with confiscated gambling equipment, Mexia, 1922. Hamer is sixth from left.

Confiscated bootlegging equipment, Mexia, 1922. Hamer is second from left.

"Winter Garden," formerly a Mexia gambling hall, raided by Hamer's Rangers, then used as headquarters during martial law.

Bootleg whiskey, captured at Mexia, 1922, by Hamer's Rangers. Hamer is at the extreme right.

Hamer and Tom Hickman beside 100-gallon still at Mexia.

Captain Hamer at target practice, Mexia, 1922.

Hamer practicing with a machine gun at Mexia.

.30-caliber model 8F autloading Remington rifle presented to Captain Hamer by the Remington Arms company in 1922. The rifle is heavily inlaid in gold and engraved with scenes from Hamer's career.

Hamer with his presentation Remington rife, after a hunting trip.

Corpus Christi home of James A. Barnes, shattered by dynamite on November 14, 1923.

Pat M. Neff, Governor of Texas 1921–1925.
John H. Jenkins Collection.

Miriam A. ("Ma") Ferguson, wife of Jim
Ferguson and twice-governor of Texas,
1925–1927 and 1933–1935.

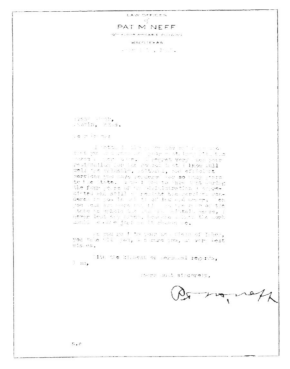

Letter to Hamer from ex-Governor Pat Neff, when
Hamer resigned from the Rangers in 1925.

Two Frank Hamers: the real one on the left, his imposter—
John B. Sawyer—on the right, San Antonio, 1926.

Captain Hamer, bottom right, and other Texas Rangers.

The Texas Rangers during the administration of Governor Dan W. Moody, 1927–1931. Hamer is sixth from left on the front row.

Dan Moody, Governor of Texas, 1927–1931.
John H. Jenkins Collection.

Hamer and Clem Calhoun at Borger.

Frank Hamer and Jim Gillette.

Rankin, Texas.

Early view of the Sherman County, Texas, courthouse, which was burned by rioters in 1930.

Scene from inside the Sherman courthouse during the Sherman riot of 1930. Hamer is the second man from the right.

Famous Texas Ranger captains. From left, standing: John A. Brooks, W. W. Sterling, Frank Hamer, John R. Hughes. Seated: Dan Roberts.

W. W. Sterling, left, and Frank Hamer, right.

Bonnie Parker and Clyde Barrow. *Wide World Photos.*

Bonnie Parker.

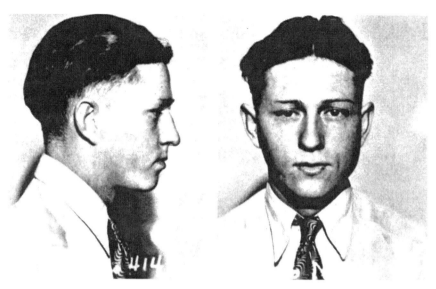

Clyde Barrow mug shots, Waco, Texas ca. 1930.

Wanted notice for Bonnie Parker, issued by the Dallas County Sheriff's Office.

Clyde Barrow and part of his arsenal.

Clyde Barrow, about 1933.

Bonnie Parker, sporting her cigar and pistol.

Buck Barrow and Clyde Barrow.

Buck and Blanche Barrow.

Clyde Barrow and Bonnie Parker.

Bonnie Parker.

Photograph taken shortly after the shooting of Buck Barrow. Blanche Barrow is at left; Buck on ground at right.

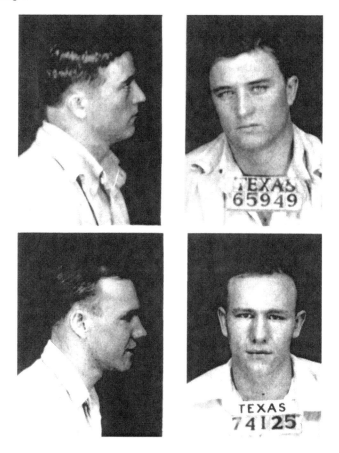

Mug shots of Henry Methvin, top, and Raymond Hamilton, bottom.

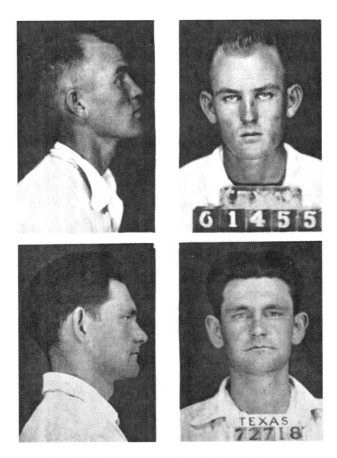

Mug shots of Joe Palmer, top, and W. H. Bybee, bottom.

Col. Lee Simmons, Texas Prison System, who requested that Hamer
be allowed to track down Clyde Barrow and Bonnie Parker.

Clyde Barrow and Bonnie Parker.

Mr, KIng — "So Raymond Hamilton nev er killed anybody. If he can
make a jury believe that I8m willing to come in and be tryed my
self. Why dont you ask Ray about those two pol icemen that got
killed near Grapevine? And while you are at it bwetter talk it
ov er with his girl friend. Bonnie and me were in missouriwhen
that happened but where was Kay?coming back from the West bankjob
wasn't he? Redhot too wasn8t he? I got it straight. And ask hi m
about that cscape at Eastham farm wherethat gard was killed.
Giess he claims he doesnt know fire any shots there don8t ge?
Well if he wasnt too dum to know how tp put a clip in a automatie
he'd hace fired a lot m ore shots and some of the vrest of the
gards would got killed too. He wrote his lawyer he was toa good
for me and didnt go my pace, well it makes a me sick to see a
yellow punk like that playing baby ed making/a jury cry over him.
If he was half as smart as me o the officers couldnt catch hi m
either/ He stuck his fingerprint on a lett er so heres mine
just to let you k now thjis is on the leve;

X Clyde

P s AsK Ray why he was so dam jumpy to get rid of those
yellow wh eels on his car and akshis girl friend how they spent easter

Letter sent by Clyde Barrow to the district attorney's office, Dallas, after
his break-up with Raymond Hamilton.

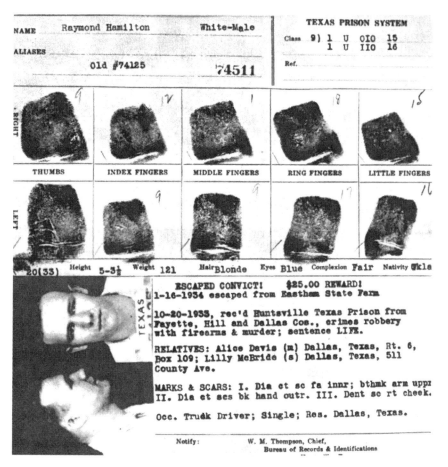

Reward notice for Raymond Hamilton, 1934.

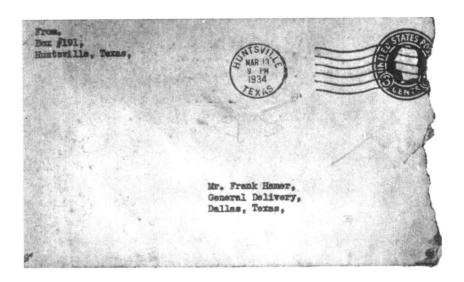

While on the Barrow–Parker case, Hamer kept in touch with Lee Simmons through a Dallas post office. These two envelopes indicate the method used.

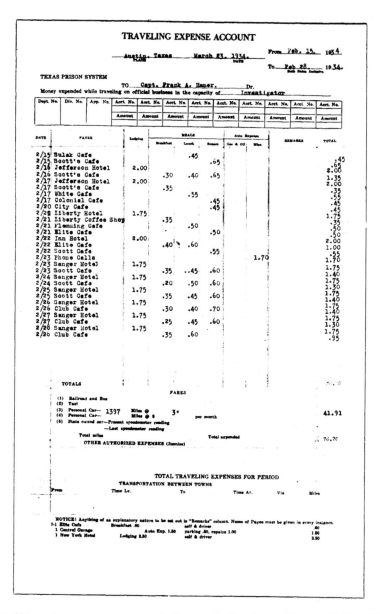

Part of Hamer's expense account on the Barrow–Parker chase, February 15-28, 1934.

E. D. Wheeler and H. D. Murphy, the two
officers killed at Grapevine, Texas, Easter, 1934.

Clyde Barrow and Bonnie Parker.

Clyde Barrow and Bonnie Parker.

WANTED FOR MURDER
JOPLIN, MISSOURI

F.P.C.29 - NO. 9
26 U 00 6

CLYDE CHAMPION BARROW, age 24 5'7",130#,hair dark brown and
wavy,eyes hazel,light complexion,home West Dallas,Texas.
This man killed Detective Harry McGinnis and Constable
J.W. Harryman in this city,April 13, 1933.

BONNIE PARKER   CLYDE BARROW   CLYDE BARROW

This man is dangerous and is known to have committed the following
murders: Howard Hall, Sherman, Texas; J.N.Bucher,Hillsboro, Texas;
a deputy sheriff at Atoka, Okla; deputy sheriff at West Dallas,
Texas; also a man at Belden, Texas.
        The above photos are kodaks taken by Barrow and his com-
panions in various poses,and we believe they are better for
identification than regular police pictures.
        Wire or write any information to the

                        Police Department.

Dallas "Wanted For Murder" notice for Clyde Barrow.

Clyde Barrow and Bonnie Parker.

Clyde Barrow with some of his and Bonnie's weapons.

Sawed-off shotgun used by Bonnie Parker.

CLYDE CHAMPION BARROW

WANTED FOR MURDER

Notify

Sheriff's Office,
Dallas, Texas.

Age 27. Ht 5-7. Wt 125
Hair Dk. Blonde
Eyes Hazel.

F.P.C.
    29 - MO 9
    26 U 00 9

Wanted poster for Clyde Barrow, 1933.

Clyde Barrow.

Frank Hamer beside the car he used in the Barrow–Parker chase.

Stolen license plates found in the Barrow–Parker death car.

The officers who participated in the killing of Clyde Barrow and Bonnie Parker. Standing, left to right: Bryan Oakley, Ted Hinton, Bob Alcorn, Manny Gault. Seated Hamer and Sheriff Henderson Jordan.

Col. Lee Simmons, left, Frank Hamer, and two reporters at Arcadia, Louisiana, May 23, 1934.

Crowds fight to get a look at the car in which Clyde Barrow and Bonnie Parker were killed, after it had been towed into Arcadia, Louisiana, on the afternoon of May 23, 1934.

Clyde Barrow's coat, on the fender of the car in which he and Bonnie Parker were killed.

Fence keeps crowd away as reporters examine Barrow–Parker death car.

Capt. Hamer and Sheriff Henderson Jordan in Arcadia, Louisiana.

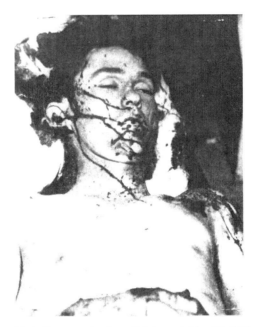

Clyde Barrow at the time of his inquest, May 23, 1934.

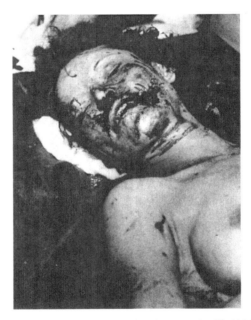

Bonnie Parker at the time of her inquest, May 23, 1934.

Walter Prescott Webb, left, interviewing Captain Hamer, top, after the Barrow–Parker chase. Manny Gault, below right, listens in.

Part of the weapons recovered from Bonnie and Clyde's death car.

Manny Gault, left, holding shotgun used by Bonnie Parker and Browning automatic rifle used by Clyde Barrow, and Captain Hamer, right, on the day they returned from Arcadia, Louisiana.

Cochton Ohio.
July 31 1934.

Capt.Hammer,
Texas Highway Patrol;
Austin Tex.

Dear Captain;

Altho I am quit late let me offer my congratulations
on your fine work in the Barrow Parker case.It
was a great relief to society to rid the county
of such a menace.

We will soon be back in Texas and would appreciate a visit if you could find time to call
on me.

Please extend my best wishes to Mr Phares and
any one else whom I might know in your department.

Sincerely yours,

Tom Mix,

Letter from Tom Mix to Hamer, July 31, 1934.

Captain Hamer and his son, Frank, Jr.

Captain Hamer and Celia Villa, Pancho Villa's daughter, during her visit to Texas.

Captain Hamer and Roy Rogers, at Rogers's home in Hollywood, California.

Mr. and Mrs. Maurice Acers, Capt. Hamer, Mrs. O. H. Davenport, actor Dale Robertson, and author Fred Gipson.

Coke R. Stevenson, Governor of Texas, 1941–1947.
John H. Jenkins Collection.

Frank Hamer and Sod Durst in an ice cream parlor in Junction. Texas.

Top, from left: Frank Hamer III; Frank Hamer, Sr.; Frank Hamer, Jr. Bottom: Mrs. Gladys Hamer and Frank Hamer III.

J. Frank Dobie, Frank Hamer, and Harry Crozier swap yarns, Austin, 1950.

16

"Let's sing a song of Borger."

In March 1926, oil was discovered in Borger, a little one-street town in the Texas Panhandle. Almost overnight, forty-five thousand oilmen, prospectors, roughnecks, panhandlers, fortune seekers, cardsharps, bootleggers, whores, and dope peddlers descended on Borger, turning it into the most corrupt and violent town the state of Texas had ever seen. It became a "no-man's land" for criminals and fugitives fleeing from the law. In a few months, the boomtown was firmly in the hands of an organized crime syndicate. Murder, robbery, prostitution, and crooked gambling flourished not only in Borger but also within the surrounding area.

Borger's bad reputation even inspired some bad poetry. An old-timer, departing for a safer home, cursed Borger with a poem that began:

> Let's sing a song of Borger,
> Famed for its graft and rot.
> It's just a wide place in the wood,
> This town that God forgot,
> For this village large boasts deeper sin,
> Than Sodom ever knew;
> Come lend an ear, kind stranger,
> And I'll whisper them to you . . .[1]

161

Early in 1927, the "old guard" of Borger petitioned Governor Dan Moody to declare martial law and send in state troops. Instead, the governor sent Frank Hamer to investigate. It took Hamer only a few days in the boomtown to send the governor a report.

"The worst crime ring I have seen in my twenty-three years as an officer," Hamer told the governor, "exists there in Borger."[2]

Hamer's investigation uncovered the fact that nearly all of the city officials, including law officers, were deeply involved with, if not actually directing, the criminal activities in Borger and Hutchinson County.

Hamer sent for reinforcements—Tom Hickman and a few other Rangers. The governor responded by ordering the mayor of Borger to put all police officials directly under Hamer's control. The mayor complied, and Hamer and the Rangers began their cleanup campaign.

"The inside of this story," reported *The State Trooper*, "would reveal that when Hamer, Hickman & Ranger Company went to Borger they found that it was more difficult to handle the officers who had flocked into the new oil town than it was to handle others. In fact, the first thing that Rangers did was to arrest about all the local peace officers and compel their resignation."[3]

Charges ranging from murder to robbery were lodged against a score of people, including local officials; and the new prosecuting attorney, John A. Holmes, began trying cases. Hamer and the Rangers were recalled to Austin.

So complete was the crime ring's control of the town that by early fall most of the ousted city and county officials had either regained their positions or had been replaced by others just as crooked. Holmes managed to hold his position, but his life was threatened several times. The threats were not taken seriously until the night of Friday, September 13, 1927, when Holmes, standing in his own backyard in front of his wife, was ambushed and murdered by an unknown assassin.[4]

Hamer and Hickman immediately left for Borger. After four days of investigation, they discovered that a signed murder confession held by Holmes was missing from his files. Hamer and Hickman questioned the man implicated in the confession and found that the theft was merely a cover-up for the murderer.

Mrs. Holmes demanded that no city or county officials be allowed to attend her husband's funeral. "Her statement," the local newspaper reported, "followed closely upon two statements from Texas Rangers investigating the case, one of which announced that the Rangers had discovered the motive for the slaying. The other announcement said that Rangers had obtained affidavits concerning an alleged plot between city and county officials."[5]

The local officials professed astonishment at this announcement. Chief of Police J. W. Crabtree announced that he would bet "one thousand dollars that when the right party is arrested the city and county officials will arrest him."[6]

Hamer refused to add fuel to the fire. "Capt. Hamer has an aversion to talking for publication," an Associated Press article stated. "'It was awfully bad.was as far as the ranger captain would go."[7] At a press conference, Sheriff Joe Ownbey told reporters that Hamer was a liar. "And you can quote me on that," he concluded.[8] Then Hamer disappeared. For three days no one saw him or heard from him. The Borger newspaper called for Hamer to come forth and prove his allegations.[9] On September 24, Hamer reappeared in Borger. He had traveled to Dallas, boarded a special train, and conferred in private with Governor Moody. The governor and Hamer rode from Dallas to Terrell, discussing the Borger situation all the way. Moody then sent word to General Wolters to meet him in Austin. Hamer continued to Brownsville, testified in a trial there, and then drove nearly a thousand miles back to Borger to continue his investigation.

On Sunday, September 29, an *Extra* hit the streets of Borger, announcing that Captain Hamer had placed Mayor Glenn A. Pace under arrest. Hamer swore out a complaint that the mayor had forced a witness in a forthcoming murder trial to leave town.[10]

On Monday, September 30, another *Extra* hit the streets. "MARTIAL LAW!" the headlines screamed. Governor Moody had declared martial law in Borger, and the Texas National Guard under General Wolters was on its way from Fort Worth. Moody's proclamation read:

"Whereas, persons sent to Borger and Hutchinson County, Texas . . . have reported to me that:

"There exists an organized and entrenched criminal ring in the city of Borger and in Hutchinson County; and that the law in said city and county is not being effectively enforced by the existing law enforcing agencies, which is the fault not of the judiciary of the county, but of peace officers . . . and that . . . there is a conspiracy between the officers and the law violators and that affidavits have been secured to the passing of money to peace officers for protection . . . and that witnesses who have been questioned concerning law violations, including the assassination of the district attorney, have been threatened and driven from the country . . . and whereas . . . there is now imminent danger of insurrection, tumult, riot and breach of the peace, and serious danger to the inhabitants . . . I do hereby declare Martial Law in said territory . . . Dan Moody, Governor of Texas."[11]

Nearly all the city and county officials were suspended from office, and most of them were jailed. The papers reported: "Col. L. S. Davidson, and five Rangers, headed by Captains Frank Hamer and Tom Hickman, took over the courthouse and jail building. Shortly after they arrived, Sheriff Joe Ownbey and a deputy arrived. They were met on the courthouse steps by Captain Hamer.

"'Where are your guns?' the Ranger asked.

"'We've already disarmed ourselves,' replied Ownbey.

"'Well, go and get them and bring them in,' Hamer ordered."[12] A court of inquiry was set up, and the Rangers and troopers got down to serious business. Newspapermen got wind that Hamer had tried to get Governor Moody to declare martial law in Borger for more than a year. They hounded him for interviews about his career until he declared that they could go to Austin if they wanted information about him.

They did and reported: "A 'deadly shot' and a 'square shooter' is the reputation of Frank Hamer, Ranger captain, whom Gov. Dan Moody has picked to 'tame' Borger."[13] Summaries of his career were then sent out over wire services across the country. Headlines claimed: "Lawless Town Feels Iron Grasp of Nervy Texas Ranger."[14] The articles did nothing to improve the tense situation Hamer faced in Borger.

Threats centered on Hamer. Bookies took bets that Hamer would be dead in less than thirty days.[15] Anonymous letters flooded the governor's office. One, postmarked Chicago, threatened both Hamer and Governor Moody.[16]

The first reports on the cleanup came from the Amarillo *Globe*: "When raids in Borger by vice squads failed all through a week of martial law to uncover liquor in any considerable quantities, Ranger Captain Frank Hamer opined there must be a nearby source of supply, eliminating need for a warehouse. Saturday (October 5) he led his force of officers and a detachment of Texas National Guardsmen into the neighboring hills and proved he was right. Two complete whiskey stills of 250 gallon capacity each, and another smaller set of paraphernalia were seized with 72 gallons of whiskey, in a raid near Electra City, three miles north of this oil town. Two women and one man were arrested.

"Raiding Saturday was the first actual participation in the anti-vice campaign by Ranger Captain Hamer. His corps of rangers, however, have made 170 arrests, of which number 59 have been charged with some crime or held for investigation."[17]

The jail was bursting at its seams. Rangers had to set up a "trotline" along the main street of Borger and handcuff their prisoners to the long chain to await the filing of charges.[18] Officers from all over the Southwest poured in to scan the faces of the fugitives to find wanted men from their territories. Lawmen paced up and down the "trotline," scanning descriptions, fingerprint files, and wanted notices. Numerous criminals were apprehended who had been hiding out in Borger.[19]

Before the end of the year, Governor Moody was able to lift the martial law. "Civil officers were ousted," one editorial concluded, "and underworld characters were given warning. They decamped. That is, they fled the city for greener pastures. Suspects were jailed. Gambling joints were dismantled. Speakeasies were unroofed. Bad men were disarmed. There was a clean-up all around. There is a new Borger. There is a happy Borger. There is a law-loving Borger. Borger has been tamed."[20]

The Austin *American* ran the following notice:[21]

Time Up

Bets made at Borger that Ranger Capt. Frank Hamer would be "bumped off in 30 days after his drastic clean-up of vice and liquor conditions there, have come due. Capt. Hamer was informed by friends that bets had been placed that he would be" dead in 30 days after he went to Borger early in October.

17

"The bankers are paying for Apaches and getting sheep herders."

In 1928, The Texas Bankers Association, one of the most powerful organizations in the state, held a meeting to discuss the alarming increase in bank robberies across the state. The bankers were exasperated not only with the growing number of robberies but also with the failure of the courts to convict or punish the criminals. The officials decided the time had come to get tough with bank robbers. The results of their meeting were posted in every bank throughout the state within a few days. Posters read:

REWARD

FIVE THOUSAND DOLLARS FOR DEAD BANK ROBBERS

NOT ONE CENT FOR LIVE ONES

The first test of the reward posters came about a month later. Late one night two men crept up to the back door of the local bank in Odessa. Just as they reached the door, four hidden officers jumped up, opened fire, and killed them both. The four officers split a reward of ten thousand dollars for their successful work.[1]

A week or two later, three Mexican bank robbers were shot down by an officer and a citizen in front of the bank at Stanton, forty miles from Odessa.[2]

Two men, Bill Brown and Charles Kilman, were killed in back of the First State Bank at Rankin, Texas. Their automobile, parked in back of the bank, was loaded with torches and other robbery equipment.[3]

The Texas Bankers Association, pleased with the decrease in robberies, paid out the reward money and considered it well spent.

Captain Hamer, however, felt uneasy about the situation. He discussed his apprehensions with Walter Webb, who later wrote:

"Shortly after the reward was posted, Captain Hamer noted that a great many bank robbers were being killed by local officers, and that practically all the killings were done in the night. Having a suspicious nature, as well as a thorough knowledge of the mental processes of both officers and criminals, he began to ask himself why so many bank robbers were killed at night and so few in banking hours. After some investigation, he came to the amazing conclusion that the men who were being killed were not real bank robbers, but simple-minded, half-drunken boys who had been induced to join pretending bank robbers, and lured to the spot where they were shot down by officers who had been tipped. The officers then collected from the bankers the five thousand dollars, which they divided with the pretending bank robbers. In short, Frank Hamer learned that two of three men were making a profession of framing robberies for the purpose of killing men at the rate of five thousand dollars a head."

"When Captain Hamer undertook legal action against the men who were engineering the killings, he could get no support from the local officers, who refused to believe that the jobs had been framed, or from grand juries that were dominated by these officers. He next approached the Bankers' Association, but with no better luck. The bankers refused to withdraw the reward, or even to modify it. Their position, and that of some officers, was that any man who could be induced to participate in a bank robbery ought to be killed. Frank Hamer does not believe in bank robbery, but he does believe in what he conceives to be right, and he holds steadfastly in the theory that every man, even a crook, is entitled to justice."

"Hamer was for a time at his rope's end. He knew that there was some way to break up the murders, but he also knew—and this gave him much concern—that other murders were being planned and that he must hurry to prevent them. He did something then that he had never done before and that he has never done since: he turned to the press. On the afternoon of March 12, 1928, he handed to the reporters in the press room of the State Capitol a signed statement containing a complete expose of what he termed the bankers' 'murder machine.'"[4]

On the morning of March 13, Hamer's story exploded in the headlines of every large newspaper across the state. His statement read, in part:

"The purpose of this article is to lay before the people of Texas, and the bankers of Texas, certain facts that they ought to have about the dead bandits and the rewards that have been paid for them. I agree that bank robbing should be stopped, that bank robbers should be shown little consideration, and should be killed when caught in the act of robbing a bank. But I do not agree that the method adopted by the Bankers' Association of Texas is either wise or just, because it is adding the crime of murder to the crime of robbery."

"There has come into existence in this state a murder machine. Here are the conditions, as I see them, out which that machine sprang and in which it is permitted by the public to exist:

"The first condition or fact is that bank robbing has become wide-spread in the last few years, not only in Texas but in other parts of the United States. There is a group of criminals who make bank, robbing a profession."

"A group of bankers representing most of the wealth of Texas combined through their association to offer a reward of $5000.00 for dead bank bandits. For one taken alive they would not pay a cent."

"This reward has aroused the greed and desire of a small group of men who have more love for money than for human life, and who are besides unscrupulous enough to do anything that will bring them money without too much risk of personal danger."

"There is another group of men, usually young men, drifters, and loafers, whose principal traits are weakness of character combined with a certain reckless spirit. These are the men who are lured by the unscrupulous ones mentioned above into bank robbery only to be shot to death by officers who have been tipped off to the robbery."

"Finally, there is the public which, because of ignorance of the true situation, gives its support to the killing of these men, not knowing the circumstances under which they are killed."

"Here is as perfect a murder machine as can be devised, supported by the Bankers' Association, operated by the officers of the state and directed by the small group of greedy men who furnish the victims and take their cut of the money. If what I have said above is true, and I shall give the facts below to prove it, THEN THE SITUATION THAT HAS COME ABOUT IN THIS STATE IS A DISGRACE TO TEXAS AND TO CIVILIZATION, AND SHOULD NOT BE TOLERATED."

"Supposed bank bandits have been killed since this reward was offered at Stanton, Odessa, Rankin, and at Cisco. The Cisco job, it will be remembered, was a daylight job and was pulled off by real bank robbers. One of the men was killed, and it will be noted that three others were taken alive. Every peace officer and citizen in Texas should commend the good work done at Cisco, and they do commend it. But what about the other three?"

"The Stanton job needs no discussion. Unfortunately the 'noble' bandit killers were better plotters than they were marksmen, and failed to kill one of the men. It was admitted that the two Mexicans were picked up, offered work, and told to wait in front of the bank, and then shot down there in the hope of collecting $15,000.00 from the Banker's Association."

"Here are some of the facts about the Odessa job where two men were killed and the reward of $10,000 paid. The job was pulled off at night. Now it so happens that it is not a capital offense to rob a bank at night—that is, without firearms and without endangering, human life. We have a private organization bringing about the execution of men by illegal means and for money. The fact that the bandit must be taken dead, and therefore tells no tales, only makes it easy for plotters to be present when the killing is done and get away under cover of darkness. This they have done and are planning to do again as I shall show later."

"The two men who were killed in the Odessa job had nothing with them that would enable them to get into the vault of the bank, once they were inside the building. The tools that were by them were 'planted' there after they were killed by a man well known to me whose name I am ready to give to the proper authorities at the proper time. This man shared privately in the reward paid by the bankers."

"The men who were killed at Odessa have been identified, and so far as fingerprints and other investigations show, there was nothing against either of them. They were not professional bank robbers, nor were they even experienced criminals. They were but weak characters who have been lured to their death in the way I have explained."

"These men did have in their possession an acetylene torch of the kind used by experienced bank robbers, but it was impossible to find either on the person of the dead men, or anywhere about, tips for this torch. Without these tips the torch was as useless to them as a flashlight without battery or bulb, as a gun without ammunition."

"The acetylene tank that was a part of the torch was stolen from a certain place which I know. The man who stole the tank left tracks made by high-heeled boots. This can be proved. But the photographs of the two dead men, copies of which I have in my possession, show that both men had on well-worn shoes. Where was the man with the boots? Was he probably not the 'expert' who was to use the torch?"

"The reward for the Rankin job was shared in by three men. But I have in my possession facts to prove that at least one other man shared in it privately. This fourth man is the same one who had a private cut in the Odessa money, is the man who has brought about the death of four men, not one of whom was an expert professional bank robber, and for this work the bankers have paid $20,000.00."

"In conclusion, I want to address a few words to the President of the Bankers' Association of Texas who heads the organization that is paying these rewards. I do not believe that the bankers of Texas or the people of Texas want to be a party to such cold-blooded murders as are being committed. The men who are dead cannot be brought to life, but my purpose is to prevent the death of others. I know it TO BE A POSITIVE FACT THAT THE MAN WHO SHARED IN THE ODESSA AND RANKIN REWARDS IS NOW FRAMING TWO MORE BANK ROBBERIES TO BE PULLED IN THIS STATE IN THE NEAR FUTURE NOT FOR THE MONEY THAT COMES FROM THE BANK ROBBED BUT FOR THE MONEY THAT WILL COME BY WAY OF REWARD FOR MEN KILLED."

"Furthermore, the reward offered by the Banker's Association has not stopped bank robbing by the professional bank robbers. Since the reward was offered, the following banks have been robbed: McCauley, Sylvester, Killeen, Copperas Cove, Mullen, Grove and Meridian. Here are seven robberies in addition to the three at Cisco, Odessa, and Rankin."

"As a duly constituted officer of the law I want to lay before the bankers of Texas a proposition, a challenge which I do not see how they can refuse to accept."

"I challenge the Texas Bankers' Association to appoint a committee for any number of their own members and let me put the facts before them that I have, and I will lay any wager that the committee will agree with me that no reward should have been paid either in the Odessa or in the Rankin job."

"I extend this appeal to the peace officers, to the press, and to the people of Texas in the hope of stopping organized murder in this state."[5]

Newspaper editorials in the following weeks debated Hamer's charges. Charges and counter-charges flew between Hamer and the bankers. The Bankers Association refused to give an inch. Hamer received a letter from a friend stating that the bankers "have already begun to get your scalp and will stop at nothing."[6]

Another friend asked Hamer how he felt about "antagonizing the greatest aggregation of wealth in the state."

"When you go fishing," Hamer responded, "what kind of fish do you like to catch, little ones or big ones? The bigger they are, the better I like to catch 'em."[7]

On April 1, 1928, Hamer had his chance to present his proof. He was called before the grand jury at Rankin to offer his evidence of the "murder machine" in Texas. The grand jury acknowledged each of his allegations and indicted two of the ringleaders. Hamer arrested the two men and obtained their written confessions.[8]

But the Bankers Association was adamant. Powerful organizations are not easily made to admit they are in error. Aside from calling Hamer a "troublemaker," the association maintained a ponderous silence. Newspapermen were refused interviews, but editorialists had a field day.

Speaking of Hamer's one-man war, the New York *Times* commented: "The reward has been denounced as contrary to public policy, calculated to incite criminal acts, and constitutes an assumption of power not vested in any organization. In no instance has a bank employee or official killed a bandit. The purpose of the reward was to encourage bankers and private citizens to resist the holdup men."[9]

Hamer himself wrote: "The situation reminds me of a story that used to be told by the Indian fighters. The Apaches and Comanches spread such terror through northern Mexico that the government offered to pay $100.00 each for Apache and Comanche scalps. Some American adventurers went to Mexico and engaged in the business and made some money. But when Apaches and Comanches became scarce, the hunters took scalps from the citizens they were supposed to protect, there being a strong resemblance between the scalp of a Mexican Indian and a Texas Apache. This is exactly what has happened in the bank scalp war. Just as it was much safer to attack a Mexican sheep herder than it was an Apache warrior, so is it much safer in Texas to shoot down an inexperienced and weak character who has been lured into the game without understanding it than to shoot down the professional bank robber. The reward is the same in either case. . . . The bankers are paying for Apaches and getting sheep herders. . . . The whole situation is one which, if it is continued, will require the cold bloodedness of a rattlesnake with a chill."[10]

The public outcry finally became so great that the bankers relented, and the terms of the rewards offered were modified according to Hamer's demands.

18

"There'll be a lot of funerals in Sherman tomorrow."

Late one night in 1927 Hamer and Hickman caused a statewide sensation by arresting two members of the Texas legislature. *The State Trooper* reported the affair:

"It seems that H. H. Moore of Cooper, Texas had introduced a bill in the Texas Legislature proposing to place a $50 State Tax on stationary optometrists. Willis W. Chamberlain, a well known optometrist of Houston, was in Austin as a Representative of the Optometry Association to work against the passage of this bill. He seemed to feel that Moore's bill was designed to 'shake down' the Optometrists for a good sum of money, and that Dale was the man who was working in conjunction with Moore. Chamberlain had some dinners with the Legislators, which he paid for, and found that he could interest Dale in his cause. It seems that Dale was to get a committee to make an unfavorable report on the bill, for which Chamberlain was to pay him $1,000 in cash, and as it turned out, all in bills."

"When Chamberlain became suspicious that Dale and Moore were in collusion to extort money from the Optometry Lobby, he went to Speaker R. L. Bobbitt of the House and laid the matter before him."

"Bobbitt communicated with Governor Moody."[1]

Moody authorized the Texas Rangers to take up the case, investigate, and arrest the guilty parties, if they found the accusations to be true. Hamer and Hickman began the investigation.

The report of *The State Trooper* continued:

"The scene then shifted to a hotel room. Chamberlain went to Moore's room, with Dale, and ordered a chicken dinner. Dale and Chamberlain left Moore's room, and as they passed out of the hotel by an alley, Chamberlain handed the money to Dale. The two Texas Ranger Captains had been informed that the 'delivery' was about to be made, and were nearby. When Dale turned to re-enter the hotel, Hamer stopped him. This story is now told in the words of Captain Hamer, who testified before a House Investigation Committee:

"'I have information,' said the Ranger, 'that you have recently accepted a bribe.' Dale denied this, but said, 'I have just accepted a fee of $1,000 to represent a man.'"

"Captain Hamer searched Dale and found the money which he handed to Captain Hickman. Dale said he could prove by a man in the hotel that everything was all right. All three men then went up to the room which was Moore's room. Hamer left Captain Hickman outside with Dale and he went inside to see Moore."

"'Has any deal of any kind been made in your room for someone to represent someone else for $1,000 or any other sum ?' Hamer asked. Moore said that there had not."

"'Do you know Dale?' asked the Ranger. Moore hesitated a minute and said he believed he did."

"'When did you see him?' pursued the Ranger. Moore said he saw him the day before, but later said he believed he had been in that evening. At the juncture, Dale and Hickman, who had been waiting outside, came into the room, and Hamer arrested Moore. The two Rangers then took the two Legislators to Court where they preferred charges against them."

"The money found on Dale was marked money. Chamberlain had gotten it from the bank, and had the cashier make four copies of the serial number of each bill. This money was examined by Hickman and Hamer the day before or shortly before it was given to Dale."

"While charges of bribery were awaiting the action of the Travis County Grand Jury, the matter was taken up in the House of Representatives. The accused men employed counsel, and made a defense, but could make no headway against the evidence of the Texas Rangers, the optometrist, and others who testified. The two men were ousted from the Legislature within a week from the time the charges were preferred. . . ."[2]

While waiting in Austin to give final testimony against the errant legislators, Hamer and Hickman used their time to capture C. E. Weston, one of the most famous bank swindlers and forgers in the United States. Weston was a wanted man in Nevada, California, and many other states on various charges of forgery and bank swindling.

Weston had gone in the print shop of E. W. Numbers in Austin and had ordered a thousand letterheads with the title "Credit Department of the First National Bank of St. Louis." Weston had given his name as "Lockwood," but Numbers had become suspicious of the customer's nervousness and reported the matter to Banking Commissioner Charles O. Austin. Austin wired the St. Louis Bank for information concerning the man and received the reply that the bank had no employee named Lockwood. Austin called Governor Moody and informed him of the peculiar circumstances, and Moody called in Hamer to investigate.

Hamer and Hickman went to the printing office and waited until Weston appeared to pick up his order. They followed him inside, but Weston became suspicious and bolted for the door. Hamer and Hickman gave chase and cornered Weston at the back of the post office. When he surrendered, he had on his person a large variety of bank letterheads and cards. The Rangers identified him as Weston by his fingerprints. Hamer and Hickman had apprehended a man who had forged thousands of dollars worth of checks, using the fake letterheads and cards as identification.[3]

In May 1930, Hamer took on one of his most frustrating assignments. George Hughes, a black man from Sherman, was accused of raping a white woman. Lynch mobs gathered, and on May 7, Sheriff Arthur Vaughn called on Governor Moody for aid. Moody called in Hamer, who rushed to Sherman with three of his Rangers. The lynch mob had swelled to more than a thousand people. The angry mob milled about in front of the Grayson County Courthouse where Hughes was confined. The district judge, R. M. Carter, had agreed to a change of venue, but had not named the place where the trial was to take place. Until he did this, Hughes was forced to remain in Sherman.

Hamer stationed his men at the back entrances of the courthouse. He faced the mob on the front steps and ordered them to disperse. The angry crowd refused to move.

"We're coming up to get him!" an agitator shouted.

"Well, if you feel lucky, come on up," Hamer replied. "But if you start up the steps, there'll be a lot of funerals in Sherman tomorrow."[4]

Hamer's words halted the mob's actions for the moment. But by late afternoon, Judge Carter still had not decided where to try the case. The lynch mob grew bolder and finally surged up the steps.

Hamer aimed low, fired two shots into the crowd, and wounded two men. Another man tried to rush up the back steps, and a Ranger shot him in the foot, thereby, as Ranger Chaplain P. B. Hill later expressed it, "discouraging other social climbers."[5]

Hamer's strongest desire was to get his prisoner back in the confines of the jail, where it would be easier to protect him. But Hughes was in deadly fear of being taken through the angry mob. Hill recounts: "His roving eyes lighted on an open vault in a corridor outside the courtroom.

"'Lock me up in there,' he pleaded, 'They can't get that open.' The vault was stout, and the door worked by a combination. They hustled the prisoner inside and slammed the door. Somebody twirled the dial."[6]

When the crowd realized Hughes was locked in the vault, they began tossing bricks through the windows. Shots were fired at the Rangers, who retaliated by tossing tear gas bombs into the crowd, with little effect. The mob poured a bucket of gasoline through the broken windows, and in a few seconds, the entire courthouse burst into flames.

Captain Hamer rushed to the judge's office to release his prisoner, but the judge and all the courthouse officials had fled for safety. No one knew the combination to the vault. Hamer rushed through the crowd, frantically searching for the judge, the district attorney, a deputy sheriff—anyone with the combination to the vault. Everyone who knew the combination had mysteriously "disappeared." Because all but a few of the town's firemen had refused to help, Hamer and his men dragged out the fire hoses and went to work.

"Some members of the crowd," Hill recalls, "cut the fire hoses. Jeering schoolboys and sullen women with babies in their arms got in the way of firemen trying to stifle the blaze. In spite of them, the flames were brought under control in time to save the courthouse—but not in time to save [Hughes]. His inert body was pulled out of the vault a while later. He had suffocated. During the night, some mobsters seized the corpse, carried joyfully into the courthouse square, and burned it on a pyre. There was more than a suspicion that some of the local authorities might have had a hand in the violence. But there was no way it could be proved."[7]

Before morning the bloodthirsty crowd was ravaging the black section of town, burning and looting in their wake. Governor Moody declared martial law and sent troops into the town. They arrested a number of mob leaders and Hamer got the murder charges filed, but sharp lawyers got nearly all the defendants acquitted of the charges. Only four men were convicted on charges of stealing a rifle from the National Guard Armory.[8] Hamer's disgust at the cowardly actions of the townspeople of Sherman never abated as long as he lived.

19

"I ain't going to take after no giant rats."

During the early 1930s, the Communist Party in the United States and a diehard remnant of the Industrial Workers of the World made a strong move to entice workers into sabotage and strikes. As the Depression hit the masses, the Communist-led organizations across the country soared in strength and support. Captain Hamer quietly initiated an investigation of Communist activities across Texas.

His investigation revealed, for the most part, that the Communists in Texas were content with their attempts to organize discontented dock and oil field workers and to pass out revolutionary literature. Numerous attempts at sabotage were tried along the East Coast, but none in Texas. In 1931, however, reports began to drift in that something more dangerous was afoot.

It began with the theft of a large amount in nitroglycerin—a much larger quantity than could ever be used by bank robbers or small-time criminal organizations. Hamer's agents, several of whom had infiltrated Texas Communist organizations, reported that oil reserves in Texas and Oklahoma were pegged for sabotage in the immediate future. The explosives had been distributed to key locations in both states.

On March 30, 1931, Hamer wrote letters to major oil companies and refineries in Texas and Oklahoma. Marked "Strictly Confidential," the letters related: "For the last several weeks I have been receiving information that there is a movement on foot among the 'Communists' or 'Reds' to dynamite oil tank farms and pipe lines . . . I consider this information reliable [and] of such importance that I deem it my duty to notify the different companies in Texas to instruct their special agents and all employees that can be trusted to be very alert and watch all movements as near as possible as to the activities of the 'Reds' with which almost all oil fields in Texas are infested."

"Only recently a large amount of nitroglycerin has been stolen in a certain section of this State, which is evidently to be used either in the above described plan or some other violation of the law. . . . Be on the alert at all times so far at least where company property is concerned."[1]

Most of the companies immediately doubled their guard. Public attention was finally aroused, when more dynamite was stolen near Seminole, Oklahoma. After the robbery, the chief of police of Seminole released Hamer's letter to the press.[2]

Hamer was enraged. All hopes of catching the Communists vanished, and the plotters—along with the stolen dynamite and nitroglycerine—went into hiding. One newspaper reported that Hamer "expressed regret couched in unvarnished language, that the public generally had been taken into his secret. He said the warnings were given in the strictest confidence."[3] Hamer absolutely refused to discuss the matter further with newspapermen.

Not only were Hamer's efforts to capture the Communist conspirators frustrated, but the publicity brought in a flood of mail from quacks. The most ridiculous one was from "Alaha," who wrote: "As head of the Seldomseens I am in position to know that there is lots of trouble ahead. Our organization is nightly doing its best to cope with the situation, but haven't as yet made much head-way. So far we have run nearly three hundred reds out of the State, but they are increasing to such an extent that it is feared that unless you Gents bear a hand very soon they will sure make trouble. Please bear in mind that this is extra work for my boys and they receive no compensation, other than being acknowledged as true RED-WHITE-BLUE men. From my scouts I have the knowledge that shortly all railroads will be put out of commission as a starter. If you wish for our cooperation we are here, and everywhere, near three thousand strong."[4]

In 1932, nearly a year later, Communists made a few futile attempts at sabotage in Oklahoma. They used both dynamite and nitroglycerin, but with the gradual easing of the Depression and with greater watchfulness on the part of law enforcement agencies, no major sabotage attempts were made in either state. Most of the stolen explosives were later recovered.

One of the last fence wars in Texas occurred about this time almost within Austin's city limits. A man purchased and fenced in some twenty thousand acres of hill country land in the Bee Cave area just out of Austin. Timberwolves, bobcats, and other predators still preyed on livestock at the time, and local ranchers and farmers would chase down the wild creatures every Sunday with their hunting dogs, for sport as well as for protection. The men agreed among themselves to erect horse gates every three-quarters of a mile along their fences to hold their chases unhampered.

The new landowner refused, and placed "No Trespassing" signs along his fences. Tempers flared on both sides, and the newcomer hired fence riders with instructions to shoot down any dogs who crossed his fences and to take a few pot shots at any trespassers as well. The neighbors retaliated by cutting the new rancher's fences. Finally, one of the fence riders took a shot at one of the poachers. The poacher returned the fire, and war was threatened. Will Brown, who had lived in the area for many years and was respected by both parties, called on Hamer for help. The two men managed to settle the domestic dispute before it got to the blood-shedding stage.[5]

About the same time as the Communist investigation, E. G. Kingsbery purchased a house that sat across a vacant, lot from the Hamer's home on Riverside Drive in Austin. The vacant lot was overgrown with weeds, and Kingsbery sent a tall, lanky black boy named Bailey to clear the lot and exterminate rats that he had seen in the house.

Thirty minutes later, Bailey was back pounding on Kingsbery's office door:

"Mr. Kingsbery, Mr. Kingsbery! I can't exterminate those rats!"

"Why the hell not?" Kingsbery retorted.

"I was just getting started," the Negro replied, "when a giant rat stuck his nose out of the weeds and snarled at me. That head must have been a foot long! I ain't going to take after no giant rats!"

Kingsbery talked Bailey into driving back to the house with him to have a look. They searched everywhere, but found no trace of a giant rat. The boy insisted he had seen one. Hamer was sitting in his yard, and the two men walked over to question him about the rats. Bailey told Hamer his story, and Hamer burst out laughing.

"That's Porky Pig, our pet javelina!" he exclaimed. "He must have wandered over to have a look at what was going on."

Hamer gave a whistle, and out trotted Porky Pig, a fat javelina. Bailey lit out for Kingsbery's car, and no amount of persuasion could get him to set foot on the lot again.

"It sho' looks like a giant rat to me," was all he would say.[6]

Porky Pig had been found by Hamer on the Callahan Ranch in South Texas. Hamer's sons—Frank, Jr., and Billy—raised him as a pet, right along with the Hamers' German shepherd dog. Porky apparently thought he was a dog instead of a javelina, and many times had proved his worth as a watchdog by treeing unwanted visitors. Porky remained one of the Hamers' favorite pets for a number of years. They finally donated him to the Brackenridge Zoo in San Antonio, where he lived out his days as one of their star attractions.[7]

Hamer was a great animal lover, and his home housed a veritable menagerie. Besides the German shepherd dog and the javelina, he kept a pet coyote named Cactus, a pet wildcat, a parrot, and a Siamese cat. One Siamese cat Hamer owned is still alive, although it is approaching eighteen years of age.

The parrot was nearly the death of Gladys on one occasion, although it seems to be her favorite pet now. She was napping one day, with a loaded pistol lying nearby. The parrot managed to escape from his cage, and curiosity got the better of him. He poked around the loaded pistol until it discharged, blasting a hole in the wall a short distance from Gladys's head.[8]

As Headquarters Captain of the Rangers, Hamer was under the immediate command of the Adjutant General's office, at that time occupied by W. W. Sterling. "My office," Sterling wrote later, "became a favorite gathering place for old timers. Included among them were several veterans whose exploits had contributed in a large measure to the fame of the Rangers. During their visits to Austin, Captain J. A. Brooks, Captain John R. Hughes, and Captain James B. Gillett always spent a great deal of time with me."

"On a summer day in 1931, I noted that both Captain Brooks and Captain Hughes were among my visitors. The two old comrades just happened to be in the city at the same time. Captain Frank A. Hamer of Headquarters Company occupied the next office. The venerable Dan W. Roberts, oldest living captain of Company D resided with one of his daughters in Austin."

"In the presence of these men, I recognized the opportunity to get a rare Ranger picture. It would never come again. Calling a photographer, we drove to the home of Captain Roberts. The old Indian fighter was very feeble in body, but his mind was clear and alert. He gave us a cordial welcome, and seemed delighted to appear in what he knew would be his last picture. We succeeded in getting the photograph of five Ranger captains who served from 1874 to 1933. They were Dan W. Roberts, John A. Brooks, John R. Hughes, Frank A. Hamer, and W. W. Sterling."[9]

In 1932, Miriam "Ma" Ferguson, wife of ousted Governor James E. Ferguson, was again elected governor of Texas. Captain Hamer immediately resigned his position as senior captain, making headlines again and adding flames to the long-standing feud between the Ranger force and the Fergusons.

Hamer had held a Ranger commission for twenty-six years. His resignation did not require his giving up his actual commission as a Texas Ranger. He merely went on inactive status. Meanwhile, Hamer's friends came to his assistance, and he was recommended for the position of U.S. Marshal for the Western District of Texas.

The campaign for Hamer's appointment was led by Senator Morris Shepherd and all the former governors of Texas under whom Hamer had served—with the notable exception of the Fergusons. Senator Tom Connally, who actually controlled the appointment, was besieged by thousands of letters from throughout the state urging Hamer's appointment.[10] Connally wrote to Hamer, however, that he had "already made a provisional commitment with respect to this place to another good friend to whom I am under tremendous obligation."[11] The other man eventually obtained the appointment, but the tremendous public support offered in Hamer's behalf was a source of great satisfaction to his family.

Governor Moody's recommendation read, in part: "By nature this gentleman is peculiarly fitted to be a peace officer. He is a man of splendid judgment. He is destitute of any sense of physical fear. He is scrupulously honest . . . I believe implicitly in his integrity and in his trustworthiness as an officer . . . Captain Hamer is in my judgment the best peace officer within the range of my acquaintance."[12]

Clem Calhoun wrote: "For ten years I prosecuted in this state and during that period of time came in contact with Frank Hamer as a peace officer. I say this, without any mental reservation, I think he is the best, most capable, and most efficient peace officer that I ever came in contact with. Time and again in the performance of his duty he has had to resort to the use of fire arms, but he has never yet fired the first shot in any such encounter. His body bears several scars nobly and honorably received in the performance of his duty as a peace officer. He has always been my ideal as a peace officer in that he has never craved publicity, but is as eager to avoid the same as the usual run of officers are to secure the same. A more noble, braver, upright peace officer never wore a gun in the State of Texas."[13]

Early in 1933, Hamer accepted a position as a special investigator for a Houston oil company at a substantial increase in salary over what he earned as a Ranger, or even what he would have earned as U.S. Marshal. He was able, however, to retain his Ranger commission and to work with other Rangers on special cases when the public safety was involved.

20

"She was—beggin your pardon—a bit of a female dog."

On Easter Sunday, 1934, William Schieffer, an elderly farmer, sat under the shade of an oak tree resting up from an unusually fine Easter dinner. He leisurely watched the string of cars drive by in front of his farm, which lay along the highway between Dallas and Grapevine. Suddenly a new Ford halted a short distance down the road from his house. The occupants, laughing and talking among themselves, tossed a whiskey bottle from the window.

Soon afterward, two highway patrolmen stopped their motorcycles and walked over to the car, which seemed to be stalled. Schieffer jumped up in horror as he saw the occupants of the car suddenly stick guns out the windows and open fire on the officers. Keeping out of sight, Schieffer crawled to the fence to get a closer look.

The car door burst open, and out stepped a small, light-haired girl with a smile on her face and a sawed-off shotgun in her hands. She walked over to one of the dying officers and stood looking down at him. Without blinking an eye, she fired two more blasts into the officer's head at point-blank range.

"Look-a-there," she exclaimed. "His head bounced just like a rubber ball!"

Laughing, she jumped back into the car and the group sped off. Schieffer ran up to the bodies, saw that both men were dead, and hurried to the highway to flag down a passing car. Soon other officers arrived with an ambulance, gathered the remains of officer E. D. Wheeler, twenty-six, and Officer H. D. Murphy, twenty-three, and slowly drove back to the Dallas morgue.[1]

Pursuing officers were unable to overtake the murderers, but fingerprints on the whiskey bottle thrown from the car were proved to be those of Bonnie Parker and Clyde Barrow.[2]

With Prohibition barely over and with the Depression in full swing, the United States was experiencing its worst crime wave. The cost of crime in the United States in 1933 was more than $13 billion.[3] During the same year, over 12,000 Americans were murdered, 3,000 kidnapped, 50,000 robbed, and 100,000 assaulted.[4] There were more homicides in Chicago alone than in the entire British Isles. Texas ranked sixth in the nation (behind Nevada, Arizona, Washington, Oregon, and South Carolina) in crime per capita, but ranked first in the number of peace officers killed. For every criminal executed, six peace officers were murdered.[5] Between 1928 and 1933, more than four thousand indictments for murder had been returned in Texas. In 1933, of 982 homicides, 685 were the direct result of gunfights.[6] Texans had ceased to strap six-shooters on their hips, but they had not ceased killing their neighbors.

It was an era of notorious criminals: Al Capone, "Pretty Boy" Floyd, "Machine Gun" Kelly, John Dillinger—and, most talked about of all, Bonnie and Clyde. Bonnie and Clyde were accused of murdering a score or more people, but only twelve people can now positively be identified as their victims.[7] Of these twelve, however, nine were law officers.

Born in Teleco, Texas, on March 24, 1909, Barrow was one of eight children of an illiterate field hand.[8] He went to school intermittently through five grades, then gave up school to join a gang of car thieves and small-time robbers. He first clashed with the law in 1926, but failed to receive a sentence until 1930.

Bonnie's girlhood was somewhat different. An honor student when she finished high school, she was born in Rowena, Texas, on October 1, 1910.[9] Her father was a bricklayer, and she had an older brother, Hubert, and a younger sister, Billie. Bonnie's life changed when she met Barrow in January 1930. They fell in love instantly, but their romance was interrupted when Barrow was jailed a month later.[10] In early March, Bonnie smuggled a pistol into his cell, and Clyde was free. He was captured a few days later and sent to Huntsville on April 21, 1930.[11]

Harrison Kinney described Bonnie and Clyde aptly: "He was a little fellow with a narrow, ratlike face. What he liked about Bonnie Parker was that her Lilliputian dimensions made Barrow seem big and strong to himself. Bonnie Parker was a mite of a thing, 4'10" tall, eighty-five pounds light, and with a tattoo on the inside of her thigh commemorating her marriage to a man serving a life sentence. She had a hard, angular little face and looked older than her twenty-two years. She read magazines of romantic confessions, painted her toenails pink, and unsettled color-conscious passers-by by trying to match her dyed-red hair with red hats, dresses, and shoes. She had a loud mouth. Until Clyde made her a full-time accomplice, she worked as a waitress. As Frank Hamer later remarked, remembering the time Bonnie had walked up to a dying motorcycle cop shot by Barrow, pushed him over on his back with her foot, and plugged him between the eyes. 'She was—beggin' your pardon—a bit of a lady dog.'"[12]

After the chase had ended, Hamer told another friend of his: "Some wild reports about Bonnie and Clyde have gained currency. Barrow drank very little and didn't use dope at all. Bonnie was cleverer and equally merciless in the matter of taking human life without provocation of any sort. She loved whiskey and kept herself stimulated with it. She couldn't carry it well, however. Every time she got too much her legs gave out. She couldn't walk. Clyde had to carry her to their car many times. That helped to identify the pair."[13]

Clyde remained in prison for nearly two years. His brother, Buck, also served a prison term, but managed to escape. In December 1931, however, Buck gave himself up and reentered prison. The Barrow family worked to get a pardon for Clyde. Nell Barrow later wrote:

"Just before Clyde was released, in a moment of despondency, despair, and utter hopelessness with life, he [Clyde] had asked a brother convict to chop off his two toes with an ax so that he would be taken within the Walls and released from drudgery in the fields. This revolting incident had just occurred when Clyde's pardon was obtained on February 2, 1932. He came home to us on crutches."[14]

Bonnie and Clyde resumed their romance and their life of crime. They started robbing grocery stores, filling stations, and small banks. Clyde expanded operations by taking in a partner, Raymond Hamilton. On March 22, 1932, they attempted a robbery, but Bonnie was captured and jailed at Kaufman, Texas.[15]

Clyde was becoming a well-known criminal in the Dallas area, and people were taking note of Bonnie as his companion. Their life of crime first made national headlines in April 1932.

Sixty-year-old J. W. Bucher and his wife Martha ran a small grocery store and filling station on the outskirts of Hillsboro, Texas. On a bright, spring morning in 1932, an attractive couple drove up to the store. The young man entered the store carrying a package under his arm.

"I've got some knives I want to get rid of, and I'll sell them mighty cheap," Clyde propositioned the grocer.

"I'm sorry, but times are tough here, and there's little demand for knives right now," the grocer replied.

Finally, after some bargaining, Bucher bought the knives, and Clyde managed to get a full view of the safe where Bucher kept his money.

Late at night on April 30, 1932, Bucher was awakened by a strident knocking on the grocery store door. Bucher stuck his head out of the second-floor bedroom window.

"Get up, old man," his caller yelled. "I want some guitar strings. You know me. I'm the boy who sold you the knives the other day."

After a few minutes of shouting back and forth, Clyde persuaded the elderly grocer to come downstairs and open the front door. Barrow gave the grocer a note—some say it was a twenty-dollar bill—for the fifty-cent purchase, and the grocer had to make change. Bucher had left his spectacles on his bedside table upstairs and called to his wife to come down and open the safe.

Martha opened the safe and took out a small drawer filled with bills and coins. When she turned around, she looked into the barrel of a revolver held by Clyde. A light-haired girl had entered the store and pulled a pistol also, pointing it at Bucher. The old man tried to grab the pistol, and Clyde opened fire. The old man fell, shot through the head. The young couple ran for the door and sped off.

Mrs. Bucher stumbled to the telephone on the wall above her husband's lifeless body. She summoned the police and then fainted. When the police revived her, the widow Bucher identified Clyde's picture.[16] Bonnie was supposedly in jail at the time, so it is probable that the girl was not she.

On June 17, 1932, the grand jury met in Kaufman and no-billed Bonnie.[17] When she arrived home, she told her mother she was through with Clyde. But, within a few weeks, she ran off to Wichita Falls. Bonnie did not return until August, according to Mrs. Parker. "They arrived early on the morning of the first, coming from Wichita Falls, where Bonnie, Clyde, and Raymond had been living in a rented cottage ever since the last of June."[18]

On August 5, Clyde, Hamilton, and several others, possibly including Bonnie, attended a dance near Atoka in the Choctaw country of Oklahoma. During the dance, Raymond and Clyde had an argument. They went outside the dance hall to fight it out.

Deputy Sheriff E. C. Moore left the barn to break up the fight. A light-haired girl who was with Barrow cursed him and slapped him across the face. He attempted to arrest her, but she ran to the car to meet Clyde and his friends. As Moore approached the car, a pistol flashed. He dropped to the ground, shot through the forehead. Sheriff Maxwell ran up and was met by a bullet also. He died four days later.[19]

The Barrow gang was on the run. They ditched their car and promptly stole another. They dropped Bonnie off at her mother's house in West Dallas just long enough to rob the Neuhoff Packing Company. They circled back, picked up Bonnie, and sped off to Oklahoma.[20]

On August 14, Nell Barrow recalls, the two families heard from their fugitive children again, "by way of the newspapers, for Clyde and Bonnie, just driving, had gone to pay Bonnie's aunt in New Mexico a visit, and had kidnapped an officer, a trick for which they later became famous. Half a dozen times within the next eighteen months Clyde kidnapped one or two policemen and took them for all-day rides before turning them loose."[21]

Accompanied by Hamilton, they swept back into Texas from New Mexico, and narrowly escaped capture in Wharton County. Mrs. Parker writes: "Clyde and Bonnie were making themselves famous, or infamous, depending on the viewpoint. Their daring escapes, their breath-taking speed, the boldness with which they came and went, were becoming legends up and down the land. Pretty Boy Floyd was crowded into oblivion; Machine Gun Kelly was an also-ran. Bonnie and Clyde had the center of the stage and were to keep it till they died."[22]

The gang drove to Michigan for a social visit with Hamilton's father. They managed to rob a few local banks, before Bonnie and Clyde left Hamilton and drifted off across the Midwest. Hamilton was turned in to the law by a girlfriend and was brought back to Texas to stand trial. He was sentenced on a number of counts, including murder, for a total sentence of 263 years and sent to the penitentiary in Huntsville.[23]

Howard Hall, an elderly ex-cowboy who ran a small grocery store in Sherman, Texas, was destined to be Bonnie and Clyde's next victim. On the evening of October 11, 1932, they entered Hall's store to buy some bread and a can of salmon. They handed clerk F. R. Little a five-dollar bill. Then Bonnie drew a pistol from her purse and ordered the two men to reach for the ceiling. Clyde reached for the money. He turned to Hall and jammed his pistol into his stomach so hard it hurt. Hall backed away, and Clyde, breaking into peals of laughter, shot him twice. The pair stayed long enough to select a few groceries, then drove off in a new-model Ford. Little identified Bonnie and Clyde's photographs, and their fingerprints offered conclusive evidence.[24]

Lumber salesman Doyle Johnson returned to his home in Temple, Texas, on December 5, 1932, and parked his car in front of the house. He sat reading the evening paper in his living room after dinner, when he heard the motor of his car being started. He jumped up and ran to the window, only to see a man driving off in his car, with a woman following in another. The salesman dashed from the house and pursued the couple. The woman fired at him, but Johnson managed to reach his car, jump aboard, and grab the thief by the neck. The driver placed a pistol against Johnson's head and fired. The salesman fell to the ground, rolled once from the car's momentum, then came to rest, his sightless eyes staring at the sky. The woman leaped from the other car, jumped in with the man, and the couple made their getaway. A few hours later, Johnson's widow and several other witnesses identified the young couple as Bonnie and Clyde.[25]

On January 6, 1933, Bonnie and Clyde were in Dallas, plotting to "spring" Hamilton, who had been transferred to the jail in Hillsboro. Local officers learned the couple were in town and attempted to bring them to justice. When Clyde drove up to the home of Mrs. Lillie McBride in West Dallas, officers were hiding near the house. Clyde walked up to the front door of the McBride house, while Bonnie waited in the car. Deputy Sheriff Malcolm Davis waited behind some shrubs as the young outlaw approached. Several other deputies waited, guns drawn, inside the house. Lillie McBride was out of the house.

A sixth sense warned Clyde of a trap. As he approached the door, he drew his gun cautiously.

"Throw up your hands and keep them up!" Davis demanded.

"Not for you or any other John Law!" Clyde yelled back, and opened fire.

Two of Clyde's slugs slammed into Davis. He fell into the bushes, dead. Clyde leaped on the running board of the car. Bonnie hit the accelerator and careened wildly off. The couple fled north to escape capture. They finally rented a small, stone bungalow in South Joplin, Missouri.[26]

Enjoying a brief respite from the law, they were joined by Clyde's brother, Buck, and Buck's wife, Blanche. Only recently released from prison, Buck, Blanche later claimed, went to Joplin to try to persuade Bonnie and Clyde to give up their lives as bandits.[27]

The foursome proved a mystery to their neighbors. They drank heavily and were quite noisy. Several complaints were filed against them. A passerby noticed a number of license plates scattered about the garage, and they were suspected of being automobile thieves. The women seldom left the house, but the men would disappear for days, often returning at dawn.[28] The neighbor's complaints to the police sent State Highway Patrolmen Kahler and Grammar down to look around. They suspected the party might be the Barrow gang, and they returned with three Joplin officers, determined to make a thorough investigation of the premises.

Just as dusk was falling on April 13, 1933, the two couples looked out on the street. The conversation suddenly ceased. Joplin Constable J. W. Harryman left his car and walked up to the garage door, level with the street. When Harryman got within ten feet of the garage door, he suddenly faced a gun. Both barrels fired, and he fell mortally wounded. Not a word had been spoken. A newspaper later reported:

"Meanwhile, Detective Harry McGinnis, was getting out of the police car, firing shots as he approached the fallen body of his comrade. Just then a window from upstairs opened, and a woman shouted:

"Pour it in 'em, Clyde. We are coming right down. Keep 'em out of the garage!"

"Clyde Barrow was doing a splendid job of it, with one man dead and another staggering."

"Detective McGrath was now firing from behind a tree. Trouper Grammer had gone to phone for reserves. Trouper Kahler was firing from behind the motor car.

Barrow was still firing steadily from behind the garage door. Now McGinnis fell, mortally wounded."

"Meanwhile, inside the garage, all was confusion. Women were racing up and down stairs bringing suitcases. The men were swearing at them to hurry. Buck Barrow was tuning up the motor car."

"Then, to the surprise of the officers, Barrow reached out, amid a rain of bullets, and pushed the dead body of Harryman to one side to make room for the car wheels to pass, and out came the bandits' car.

"Inside the car were the outlaw Barrow brothers and Bonnie Parker, also Blanche Barrow, wife of Buck Barrow."

"Clyde Barrow was at the wheel, as usual, a notoriously fast—and good— driver. Machine guns and revolvers were pouring a rain of bullets on the officers, most of whom were now behind trees and proceeding with caution. The bandit's car sped down the concrete road toward the wilds of Oklahoma. With their usual run of luck, Bonnie and Clyde had gotten away, leaving death and sorrow behind them."

"The place was carefully searched, and a poem entitled 'Suicide Sal,' only partly finished, was found. A newspaper man also found, and had developed, a roll of film which showed Bonnie Parker holding a heavy pistol and smoking a big cigar. Other pictures in the same roll showed Clyde Barrow with a brace of guns standing in front of his motor car, also a picture showing Bonnie in the act of holding up Clyde with a sawed-off shotgun, while she reached for a revolver held in his belt."[29]

Because of their sensational poses, the confiscated pictures made the front pages across the country. Thousands were amended to "Wanted" circulars. Millions of people began to recognize Bonnie and Clyde. The newspapers latched on to the picture of Bonnie holding the heavy pistol and smoking the cigar, and quickly labeled Bonnie as Clyde's "cigar-smoking gun moll."

In letters to and talks with her mother, Bonnie later denied vehemently that she smoked cigars, swearing that she had posed for this picture with one of Clyde's cigars in her mouth as a joke.[30] However, those who lived through the era remember her as a confirmed cigar smoker.

On June 11, 1933, Bonnie and Clyde were driving at their usual breakneck speed north of Wellington, Oklahoma, when they missed a detour sign and plunged over an embankment into the Salt Fork of the Red River. Neighboring farmers came to their aid and treated Bonnie, who was burned and badly injured. The woman who nursed Bonnie was paid for her troubles by being shot in the hand. One of the farmers escaped and brought Sheriff George Corry and Marshal Paul Hardy, but the two officers were captured, taken on a wild ride, and left handcuffed together and bound with barbed wire to trees near Erick, Oklahoma. Both officers suffered severely but were found before it was too late.[31]

June 23, 1933, marked the Barrow gang's next murder. After robbing a grocery store in Fayetteville, Arkansas, Bonnie and Clyde fled down the highway into the mountain country near Alma. Town marshal H. D. Humphrey received a telephone call, warning him to be on the lookout for the couple driving a small, tan Ford. When Humphrey spotted the car tearing into town, he rushed out, yelling to the couple to halt. One of the two leaned out the window, took aim, and fired point-blank at the officer, killing him instantly.[32]

On July 28, 1933, the Barrow gang was holed up in a motel near Platte City, Missouri. When other residents became suspicious, police surrounded the motel. After a wild shooting spree, the fugitive escaped, but with Buck mortally wounded. Police caught up with them, had another shoot-out, and took Buck and his wife into custody. Buck died shortly thereafter, but Bonnie and Clyde managed to escape, despite serious wounds.[33]

While the gang was fleeing from justice, Clyde's running mate, Hamilton, remained in prison. Although Hamilton and Clyde had come to blows several times over Bonnie's affections, both Bonnie and Clyde hoped to help him escape.

Hamilton's prison record states that he was five feet, three inches tall and weighed 121 pounds. It lists his civil occupation as "truck driver," and his habits as "temperamental." The prisoner was serving a life sentence at Eastham State Farm near Huntsville for "robbery with firearms, robbery, and murder."[34]

By means of a third party, Clyde got word to Hamilton that he would try to help him escape on January 16, 1934. A plan of action was worked out, and Clyde offered to help as many escape as he could carry in his car. On the morning of January 16, guards Major Crowson and Clem Bosnian led the prisoners out into the cotton fields along the Trinity River Valley. Unnoticed, one of the convicts, Joe Palmer, slipped behind a log. Clyde had secreted a .45-caliber automatic pistol behind a log the night before. When Palmer had it safely in his hand, he shouted, "This is a break! Don't you guards make a move, or we'll let you have it!"[35]

Hamilton, Henry Methvin, Palmer, W. H. Bybee, and one more prisoner backed away from the surprised guards. Hamilton reached under the log and drew out another .45. Bonnie and Clyde drove along the highway besides the prison farm. Someone started shooting. In a barrage of nearly one hundred shots fired by Palmer, Hamilton, Bonnie and Clyde, one of the guards lurched forward dead. Clyde and Hamilton later argued over who killed the man but the escape was a success.[36]

Lee Simmons, head of the Texas prison system, was enraged over the escape and the senseless killing of the guard. In his book, *Assignment: Huntsville,* he described his actions:

"It was not too difficult to reconstruct what had actually happened on that morning of January 16, 1934. Most of the details of the escape plot were obtained from information given by an ex-convict, James Mullin, alias Jimmie Lamont. Mullin had been released recently from Eastham Farm. But he had served time in eight different penitentiaries, and we were so sure that he was somehow mixed up in the break that we promptly had him picked up."

"Mullin was already in trouble again, having stolen some guns and ammunition from a federal armory. Thus he was sure of imprisonment again. . . . Mullin didn't like to work, and he had already had a taste of labor as it is required on Eastham Farm. Accordingly he struck a bargain with us, if we would let him serve his next term at the federal prison, instead of at Eastham Farm, he would tell us what he knew about the break. We figured we needed help in the form of information more than Mullin needed a choice of prisons, so we agreed. His story was substantially as follows:"

"Upon being discharged from Eastham, Mullin had agreed to go to Dallas on behalf of Hamilton and Palmer to tell Floyd Hamilton, Raymond's brother, to get in touch with Clyde Barrow and ask him for help in the break, which had already been planned in detail. Barrow at once fell in with the plan, and further details were worked out. Clyde and Raymond had a west Dallas pal in Fred Yost, then a trusty around the yard at Eastham Farm, who helped with their arrangements."

"On the Sunday afternoon before the Tuesday break, Floyd Hamilton came down to the farm to visit Raymond and confirmed the plan in detail. The next morning around two o'clock, Floyd Mullin placed two loaded automatics under a small culvert near the wood yard. . . . The break worked out exactly as planned, with the exception of Bybee's joining the party. Palmer vouched for Bybee to Clyde as being safe, since he was a life-termer. Three of the four fugitives crawled into the turtleback of the car. Clyde, Bonnie, and Mullin rode in the seat, and Raymond Hamilton rode in Mullin's lap."

"I went on thinking and planning ways to bring all four to justice. I lay awake nights until I worked out what I felt to be a feasible plan. It involved a great deal of detail and would require the fullest confidence to be reposed in me by my superiors. In particular it had to have the fullest assistance of the Governor."

"First I requested the prisoner board to create a new position, Special Investigator for the Texas Prison System. This could be done under the law, with the approval of the Governor, the Chairman of the State Board of Control, and the Comptroller of Accounts. After I had explained my plan, the Board and other necessary officials granted my request."

"I told the Board that I wanted to hire an experienced and dependable person to put on the trail of Clyde and Bonnie and to stay on it until they were either captured or put out of business. Board members asked me who this person could be, and I answered that I did not yet know but that when I had made up my mind I did not intend that they or anybody else should know who he was."

"I had my eye on one or two former Ranger Captains. I weighed my choice strictly on the basis of who would be the best man for the job. Barrow was a desperado with no regard for human life, a man who despised the law and hated all peace officers. Whoever stopped Clyde Barrow would do so at the risk of his life. I knew from what Bybee and James Mullin (and after his capture, Palmer) told me that Barrow had made up his mind never to be taken alive and that Bonnie Parker was determined to go down with Clyde. That was the kind of game we had to hunt; it was my task to find a hunter of the kind to handle it."

"My decision was for Frank Hamer. I talked to nobody about it, but my own mind kept telling me that Hamer was the man. I had known him and his career for thirty-odd years. But I also knew that there was bad feeling politically between Hamer and the Governor. So before discussing the matter with Hamer or anyone else I went to Governor Miriam Ferguson and former Governor Jim Ferguson."

"The Fergusons agreed to help me in any way that was right and proper. They had already assigned certain rangers to the job and were going to offer a $1,000 reward for Clyde Barrow, alive or dead. I told them of my need for a special investigator and that I was considering Frank Hamer. Did they have any objections?"

"'Frank is all right with us,' spoke up Governor Miriam. 'We don't hold anything against him.'"

"Hamer would be helped from the underworld, and I was being approached by several of Barrow's former associates, both in the penitentiary and on the outside, who were offering to help put Clyde and Bonnie on the spot."

"'I might want to put somebody on the ground,' I told the Governors, meaning that I might want to promise someone clemency. 'But that would have to be after he made good, and not before. You will have me between you and the public; it will be on my recommendation that you grant clemency, if my man makes good.'"

"'Go ahead,' said former Governor Jim, speaking first. 'Go ahead. I told you we would do anything you want to assist you.'"

"Is that all right with you, Governor?' I asked, turning to Governor Miriam. After all, she was the one legally empowered to act.

"'Yes, that is all right with me,' she answered."

"From the gubernatorial office I went straight to Hamer. I told him what I had in mind—to take Clyde and Bonnie off the road. I needed his help, and I told him why. I told him that his name had been mentioned only to the Fergusons and that they were agreeable to the assignment. I said I would put him completely in charge and back him to the limit."

"How long do you think it will take to do the job?' he asked. That was his way of indicating that he had no intention of jumping into something that might peter out under him. He knew that the FBI, the Texas Rangers, and a great many peace officers had been trying unsuccessfully for years to run down, capture, or kill Clyde Barrow. Hamer was not about to accept an arrangement, whereby, after a few months I might say, 'Well, it looks like we are not getting anywhere, so we might as well call it off.'"

"That's something no man can guess,' said I. 'It might be six months; it might be longer. Probably it will take you thirty days to get your feet on the ground before you start to work. No matter how long it takes, I will back you to the limit.'"

"'Well,' Hamer said, 'if that's the way you feel about it, I'll take the job.'"[37]

21

"Someday they will get me, but it won't be without resistance."

Now the nation's most famous lawman was on the trail of the nation's most wanted criminal. Hamer took the job strictly from a sense of personal duty. He was earning more than $500 a month working for a Houston oil company—a healthy living for 1934—and his salary from the State of Texas would be only $180 per month.[1] The cut in salary would be a strain on his family, and the search might take a long time. Hamer knew that he was fifty years old, and that his family would be in dire circumstances should he be killed or incapacitated while trying to apprehend the fugitives. And, further, he did not like working under the Fergusons, whom he despised.

But more than he hated the Fergusons, he hated the idea of two insane murderers running loose. Our present era tends to scoff at heroism and to look for ulterior motives in any heroic deed. Yet, in all of American history, no lawman ever faced more dangerous criminals, and no lawman ever held more unselfish, heroic motives, than did Captain Hamer when he set out to bring in Bonnie and Clyde.

After the chase was finally over, Captain Hamer sat down with his friend, the Ranger historian Webb and told him exactly what had happened. The interview with Webb on July 4, 1934, was the only time Hamer ever opened up about his long chase. He told Webb:

"I was not in the state service, having resigned from the Texas Rangers on November 1, 1932, because Miriam A. Ferguson and her husband were soon to take charge—for the fourth time—of the Governor's office. About February 1, 1934, Lee Simmons, superintendent of the penitentiary, came to Austin and asked me if I would be willing to take Barrow's trail and follow it to the end. I agreed to try it, and was issued a commission as a state highway patrolman. The fact I was after Barrow was known to only a few people before we caught him."

"On February 10, I took the trail and followed it for exactly 102 days. Like Clyde Barrow I used a Ford V8, and like Clyde I lived in the car most of the time."

"I soon had valuable sources of information, but these cannot be revealed without violating confidences. The fact that I never betray a confidence, even from the criminal, has resulted in bringing me inside information which every successful officer must have. I soon learned that Barrow played a circle from Dallas to Joplin, Missouri, to Louisiana, and back to Dallas. Occasionally he would vary the beat, but he always seemed to return, as most criminals do. One time, he and Bonnie went as far east as North Carolina for no other purpose, it seems, than to visit a cigarette factory. Again they would go to Indiana, Iowa, or New Mexico, but like wild horses, they would circle to their old range. The thing to be decided was whether to set the trap in Texas, Missouri, or Louisiana, because he was "hot" in Texas and in Missouri, having killed men in both states, but he had killed no one in Louisiana, and would probably make that his hiding place."

"It was necessary for me to make a close study of Barrow's habits. I had never seen him, and never saw him until May 23, but I interviewed many people who knew him, and studied numerous pictures of him and his woman companion. I knew the size, height, and all the marks of identification of both Clyde and Bonnie. But this was not enough. An officer must know the mental habits of the outlaw, how he thinks, and how he will act in different situations. When I began to understand Clyde Barrow's mind, I felt that I was making progress. I learned that Barrow never holed up at one place; he was always on the go; and he traveled farther in one day than any fugitive that I have ever followed. He thought nothing of driving a thousand miles at a stretch. Barrow was also a master of side roads, which made his movements irregular. Around Dallas, Joplin, and in Louisiana, he seemed to know them all."

"Before the chase ended, I not only knew the general appearance and mental habits of the pair, but I also had learned the kind of whiskey they drank, what they ate, and the color, size, and texture of their clothes. I first struck their trail at Texarkana. At Logansport they bought a half-gallon of whiskey; near Keechi they bought gasoline, and then went in the night to a negro house and had the negroes cook them some cornbread and fry a chicken. In Shreveport they bought pants, underwear, gloves, and an automatic shotgun. In their camp on the Wichita River, near Wichita Falls, they lost or threw away some bills for goods bought in Dallas. From the clerk I learned the size, color, and pattern of one of Bonnie's dresses, and the kind of Ascot tie and belt buckle she wore. A description of these was sent to Ed Portley of Joplin, Missouri, with information that Clyde and Bonnie were probably hiding in some abandoned mines near by."

"But the trail always led back to Louisiana, where I located their hideout on February 17. I cannot give the name of the parish because of what followed. Because I was out of Texas, it was desirable for me to take the local officers into my confidence. I learned that the sheriff of this parish could not be trusted, and so it was arranged to have Barrow's hideout moved into a parish where the officers were more reliable. In a comparatively short time the hideout was established in Bienville Parish at a place well known to me."

"The next task was to catch Clyde when he was 'at home'. On several occasions I went alone to this secret place. It was my hope to take him and Bonnie alive; this I could do only by finding them asleep. It would have been simple to tap each one on the head, kick their weapons out of reach, and handcuff them before they knew what it was all about. Once the plan came near succeeding, and would have succeeded but for one of those accidents which will happen over which the officer has no control. There was always plenty of sign in the camp; stubs of Bonnie's Camels—Clyde smoked Bull Durham—lettuce leaves for their white rabbit, pieces of sandwiches, and a button off Clyde's coat. I found where they had made their bed."

"The end would have come two or three weeks earlier had not some local and federal officers made a drag on Ruston, Louisiana, and when Clyde heard of it, he quit the country and I had to wait for him to return."[2]

About this time Clyde and Hamilton came to a parting of the ways. Some say they parted company over Bonnie's affections. Some say Raymond wanted to break away to form his own gang. Mrs. Parker states:

"Raymond was out after big dough. He was not content to rob filling stations and live from day to day. He wanted a lot of money and to live in style. When Clyde refused to rob any more banks for a while, Raymond started in alone. . . . After the split, Raymond wrote a letter to his lawyer in Dallas, for the press, in which he, in effect, requested all police officers to take note and put down in their books that Raymond Hamilton was a gentleman bandit, in no way to be connected with Clyde Barrow, desperado, and that he was not operating with Clyde any more. . . . This burned Clyde up, and he wrote one in reply."[3]

Clyde sent his letter, signed and sealed with his fingerprint, to the District Attorney of Dallas:

"So Raymond Hamilton never killed anybody. If you can make a jury believe that I am willing to come in and be tried myself. Why don't you ask Ray about those two policemen that got killed near Grapevine? And while you are at it better talk it over with his girl friend. Bonnie and me were in Missouri when that happened, but where was Ray? Coming back from the West bank job, wasn't he? Red Hot, too, wasn't he? I got it straight. And ask him about that escape from Eastham Farm where that 'gard' was killed. Guess he claims he didn't fire any shots there, don't he? Well, if he wasn't too dum to know how to put a clip in a automatic he'd have fired a lot more shots and some of the rest of the gards would got killed too. He wrote his lawyer he was too good for me and din't go my pace, Well it make me sick to see a yellow punk like that playing baby and making a jury cry over him. If he was half as smart as me the officers couldn't catch him either. He stuck his fingerprint on a letter so here's mine too, just to let you know this is on the level, (signed) Clyde."[4]

Clyde also wrote to Hamilton, cursing his old friend and running mate. "I know that someday they will get me," Clyde wrote, "but it won't be without resistance."[5] He made no bones about his and Bonnie's killings.

Bonnie and Clyde drove back to Texas, and on Easter Sunday, April 1, 1934, shot the two highway patrolmen, E. D. Wheeler and H. D. Murphy. Parker's mother later wrote:

"We weren't to see them again till a week after the Grapevine killing on April 1, 1934. The real reason back of that Grapevine murder is such a simple thing that the telling of it borders on the ridiculous. All the newspaper stories were wrong. The reports were that Raymond Hamilton, who had just robbed the bank at West, Texas, was to join Clyde and Bonnie on this side road. Clyde and Raymond hadn't been together for weeks, and there was no chance of their meeting this day. They were not parked there waiting for any gangsters. They had come to Dallas because Bonnie had a white rabbit which she wanted me to have for Easter, and they were waiting for both families to join them when the two officers drove up and were killed."[6]

So officers Murphy and Wheeler met their deaths, according to Mrs. Parker, because they prevented Bonnie from giving her mother an Easter bunny.[7]

Lee Simmons had a different theory: "On April 1 the radio broadcast went out reporting Hamilton's robbery of a bank near West, Texas. Barrow was sure that he could anticipate his former partner's next move. For it was Hamilton's established practice, after having pulled a job, to head as directly as possible for the area of unpaved country lanes north of Grapevine, in the vicinity of Roanoke, there to lie up while pursuit swept by. This time Clyde and Bonnie reached the area ahead of him and parked their Ford a short distance off the Grapevine highway at a point which Hamilton was expected to pass. It was a bright, clear Easter morning. . . . William Schieffer, the farmer near whose home this killing took place, told me that he had been watching the car for some time because it had stayed there so long. He saw the entire occurrence. Bonnie's victim fell and was lying on his side. She walked over to the prostrate patrolman, put her foot on his body, and pushed him over so that he lay on his back. Then cold-bloodedly she stepped back a few feet, fired another shot into the body, turned and ran to the Ford."

"Hamilton, who was indeed proceeding toward the place where Barrow waited in ambush, had bogged down on a country road, a delay which undoubtedly saved his life. Unable to get out of the mud, he kidnapped a farm woman, Mrs. Cam Gunters, leaving her four year-old son in the road. The next morning he released her in Houston."[8]

"These murders," Hamer told Webb, "brought the total number charged against them to fourteen, shortly raised to fifteen. As a result of these repeated crimes, the whole state was aroused and every peace officer and highway patrolman was on the lookout for the pair."[9]

Clyde, Bonnie, and Henry Methvin fled to Oklahoma. On April 6, after a rainstorm, their car stuck in the mud near Miami, Oklahoma. Sixty-three-year-old Constable Cal Campbell and another officer drove up to see if he could help them.

"You folks seem to be in need of some help," he said, as he walked up to the car.

"We don't need any help from the laws!" Bonnie yelled.

"We'll be glad to help pull you out," Campbell offered.

With that, Clyde pulled his shotgun, fired, and Campbell fell dead. Bonnie and Methvin opened fire on policeman Percy Boyd, who was sitting in Campbell's car. They wounded Boyd in the forehead, then forced him to help pull their car from the mud. Boyd was taken on a wild, fourteen-hour ride before being released.[10]

Bonnie's mother wrote: "On Saturday, April 6, less than a week from the Easter killing, Clyde, Bonnie, and Henry were again in the papers. This time they had killed Constable Cal Campbell at Commerce, Oklahoma, and had kidnapped the police chief, Percy Boyd. We believed that story because it sounded just like them. But we didn't learn details till a week later when Clyde and Bonnie came back to Texas . . . Bonnie and Boyd struck up quite an acquaintanceship. He told her about his family and she told him about hers. She also asked him if anything happened to her while he was in the car, would he see that her mama got the white rabbit? Boyd promised."

"'We liked him,' Bonnie said. 'When we let him out, we gave him a new shirt and tie and expense money back home. He asked me: 'Bonnie, what shall I tell the world when I go back?' And I said, 'Tell them I don't smoke cigars!' He did it too. It was in all the Oklahoma newspapers.' This pleased Bonnie greatly."[11]

Meanwhile, Hamer was on their trail. His story continues:

"I traveled alone until shortly before the middle of April. On April 10, I called Chief L. G. Phares of the Highway Patrol to tell him that Barrow had used a Pontiac sedan to make his getaway after killing Constable Cummings and kidnapping the chief of police of Commerce, Oklahoma. I gave Chief Phares the license and engine number of this car and also the numbers on extra license plates from Oklahoma and Louisiana which Clyde carried in his car. Chief Phares told me that the Highway Department had decided to hire an extra man to travel with me. I asked for B. M. Gault who had served with me in the Headquarters Ranger Company. Gault met me in Dallas on April 14, and traveled with me until the chase ended on May 23."

"Bob Alcorn and Ted Hinton, from the sheriff's department of Dallas, gave me information, and were members of the party that met Barrow. In Louisiana I made contact with sheriff Henderson Jordan of Bienville Parish, and after I had informed him of my plan, he agreed to assist me and pay no attention to other officers, state or federal. He brought with him Deputy Oakley."

"We did not find Barrow at his hideout but at his 'post office'. All criminals who work in groups must have some way of communicating with one another when they get separated. I learned that Clyde had his post office on a side road about eight miles from Plain Dealing, Louisiana. It was under a board which lay on the ground near a large stump of a pine tree. The point selected was on a knoll from which Bonnie in the car could command a view of the road while Clyde went into the forest for his mail."

"By the night of May 22, we had good reason to believe that Clyde would visit this mail box within a short time. About midnight we drove out to Gibsland, secreted our cars in the pines, and made arrangements to furnish him more news than he had ever received at one time. No detail was neglected. The road here runs north and south, and the knoll over which it rises is made by a spur of point which slopes from east to west. The stump that marked the location of the post office is on the west side of the road. We therefore took our position on the opposite, and higher, side so that we could look down on the car and its occupants. Within an hour after we reached the place, which was about 2:30 in the morning, we had constructed a blind from pine branches within about twenty-five or thirty feet of the point where the car would stop."

"We expected Barrow to come from the north, or from our right as we faced the road. The six men were spaced at intervals of about ten feet, parallel to the road. I held the position on the extreme left, and next was Gault, Jordan, Alcorn, Oakley, and Hinton in the order named. Gault, Jordan, and myself were to take care of the front seat, Oakley and Alcorn of the back seat, if occupied, while Ted Hinton at the end of the line represented the reserves."

"We agreed to take Barrow and the woman alive if we could. We believed that when they stopped the car, both would be looking toward the post office and away from us; such action on their part would enable us to escape observation until we demanded their surrender."

"With everything ready, we had nothing to do but wait about seven hours, without breakfast or coffee. Waiting is about the hardest thing an officer has to do. Many men will stand up in a fight, but lose their nerve completely if required to wait long for the excitement. On this occasion I did not detect the slightest nervousness on the part of a single man."

"As daylight came a few cars passed, and occasionally a logger's truck; and the sun came up at our back, which was in our favor. It was probably about 9:10 when we heard a humming through the pines that was different from that made by the other motors. A car was coming from the north at a terrific speed, singing like a sewing machine. We heard it when it must have been three miles away."

"Finally, it came into view at a distance of a thousand yards, and though it was still coming rapidly, it began to slow down as it climbed the hill toward us. We first recognized the color of the car, a gray Ford sedan, then the license number; we saw two persons, a small black-headed man and a small red-haired woman. We recognized Bonnie and Clyde, and knew there was no mistake. The speed continued to slacken under the brakes and the car came to a full stop at the exact spot that we had previously decided it would."

"When Barrow brought the car to a standstill, he pressed the clutch and slipped into low gear with the engine idling. Just as we had figured, both he and the woman peered with all their attention toward the stump."

"At the command, 'Stick 'em up!' both turned, but instead of obeying the order as we had hoped, they clutched the weapons they either held in their hands or in their laps."[12]

Clyde grabbed his 10-gauge shotgun. Bonnie brought up her sawed-off shotgun. Hamer said when Bonnie stuck her gun at him, it was "like looking down the Holland Tunnel."[13]

Hamer was completely in the open. He stood in the road just a few yards from the killers. When they turned their guns on him, he realized he could never take them without a fight. He opened fire with his .35-caliber autoloading Remington rifle, with a special twenty-round magazine.

"When the firing began," Hamer recalled, "Barrow's foot released the clutch and the car, in low gear, moved forward on the decline and turned into the ditch on the left. I looked at my watch and it was 9:20."[14]

Hamer's first shots hit both Bonnie and Clyde. "Bonnie," one of the officers recalled, "screamed like a panther."[15] When the car jerked forward, the other officers jumped up and fired, riddling the car and raising a thick cloud of dust.

The car stopped and Hamer walked toward it. "Be careful, Cap!" Gault cautioned. "They may not be dead."[16]

With his .45 Colt automatic pistol on the ready, Hamer approached the car. The dust began to settle, and Hamer looked in. Bonnie and Clyde had fought their last gun battle. Hamer stuck the pistol in his belt, leaned the Remington rifle against the car, and opened the front door. Clyde fell to the ground. His shotgun and Hamer's Remington fell across his body. Bonnie slumped forward, her head between her nees.[17]

Hamer looked down at the girl. "I would have gotten sick," he commented later, "but when I thought about her crimes, I didn't. I hated to shoot a woman—but I remembered the way in which Bonnie had taken part in the murder of nine peace officers. I remembered how she kicked the body of the highway patrolman at Grapevine, and fired a bullet into his body as he lay on the ground."[18]

Hamer's men poured over the automobile. "The examination," he recalled, "revealed that the car was nothing but an arsenal on heels. The inventory included:

3 Browning automatic rifles	Cal. 30
1 sawed-off shotgun	Gauge 10
1 sawed-off shotgun	Gauge 20
1 Colt automatic pistol	Cal. 32
1 Colt automatic pistol	Cal. 380
1 Colt revolver, double action	Cal. 45
7 Colt automatic pistols	Cal. 45
100 machine gun clips of 20 cartridges each	
3000 rounds of ammunition scattered all over the car."[19]	

While the shooting was taking place, a logging truck drove over a ridge to the north. The driver and two black helpers on the back of the truck saw the bullets kicking up dust and ricocheting off the car. They dove for the brush just off the road. When the shooting died down, the driver cautiously peered out, then walked over to the officers. But it took him nearly an hour of coaxing and bribing before the black helpers would come back out of the brush.[20]

22

"One man wanted to amputate Barrow's trigger finger."

Hamer left the other lawmen at the scene of the shooting and drove to nearby Arcadia to locate a telephone. He found that the only telephone in town was at the central office, and he asked the operator to call Simmons in Huntsville. At ten o'clock he contacted Simmons, and with the telephone operator listening in astonishment, he told his boss he had finished the job. Then Hamer placed a call to his wife to tell her he was safe. Simmons and other law enforcement officials left immediately for Arcadia. Hamer returned to the scene of the shooting and found to his astonishment that nearly two hundred cars were parked along the narrow dirt road. People crowded around the death car, morbidly curious to see for themselves the results of Hamer's trap. Some walked up to the car, peered in, and turned away sickened. Others giggled nervously. A wrecker arrived from Gibsland, eight miles away, and towed the bullet-riddled car to Arcadia. Crowds as large as six thousand fought with one another to catch a glimpse of it.[1]

The once-slumbering hamlet was a beehive of activity. One report stated:

"People in little lots on every corner, people huddled on every sidewalk, unmindful of the rain showers; people, people everywhere—all breathing the proverbial sigh of relief because of the death of Clyde Barrow and Bonnie Parker

. . . . Harassed officers, busy undertakers, thriving restaurant men—these were about the only citizens in this little community of 2,500 who weren't dropping all else to comment favorably on the killing of Barrow and the Parker girl. Every merchant who possibly could closed his doors or got a helper in his place and joined the throngs clustered about the little furniture store which housed the town's undertaking parlor, about the Bienville Parish Court House, about the spot out from Gibsland, west of here where the two outlaws met their death."

"Frank Hamer, who has been working for the last three months exclusively on the Barrow-Parker case, apparently was the leader of the group. But, modestly, he refused to take credit."[2]

Simmons arrived in Arcadia that afternoon. He later recalled:

"A large crowd had gathered at the parish jail by the time I reached Arcadia. Many newspaper reporters had flown in at the first flash on the radio. As I walked up and shook hands with Captain Hamer and his fellow officers, Hamer turned to the newsmen: 'Now, here's the boss. I've been acting on his instructions. If any statement is to be given out, he is the one to make it."

"Actually, of course, Hamer was his own boss. He deserved to be. But he was carrying out his lifetime policy of taking small credit for his accomplishments. As the newspaper people grabbed me and peppered me with questions, I realized that they were entitled to some information, so I went as far as I felt I could give them the story."

"I told them of the employment of Captain Hamer and of the subsequent assignment of Gault, Hinton, and Alcorn to the job. The reporters already knew something of this, but they had known nothing of the important part played by Sheriff Henderson Jordan, which I now revealed to them. But the Methvins? How about them?"

"'There are some things,' I finally said, 'which the public is not entitled to know.' Would I state that the Methvins had nothing to do with the ambush? I stood pat on my statement and refused further comment. As a matter of fact, Henry Methvin had known nothing of the deal made with his father until the morning of April 22, when Clyde and Bonnie made their last call at Methvin's house in the woods."[3]

Hamer and Simmons broke away from the reporters and walked over to the Barrow car. Hamer unlocked it and said, "Here is what's in it. It's up to you to see what's done with it."

"No," Simmons told him. "You take what you want. I'm not entitled to anything. You take charge of it and handle it."[4]

Coroner J. L. Wade impaneled a special jury to hear the testimony of the six officers. It took more than an hour to get all the details. Wade asked Hamer if he was satisfied that the slain couple was Barrow and Parker. Hamer replied, "Yes." Then, he added:

"If you will pull off his left shoe, you'll find his big toe is cut off. He had this done when he was in a prison farm to keep from working. Also, he has a tattoo with the initials 'E B W' on his left arm, and on the right arm is a figure of a girl with the name 'Grace' tattooed there."

"If you will look at her right thigh, you'll find that she has a double heart with an arrow tattooed through them with the name 'Bonnie' tattooed on one heart and the name 'Roy' on the other."[5]

The coroner and Dr. J. M. Moseley, along with other members of the jury, examined the bodies and found them to be so marked. It was brought out at the inquest that Bonnie was wearing two diamond rings, one gold wedding ring on the third finger of her left hand, one small wrist watch on her left wrist, a three-acorn brooch on her breast, and a cross around her neck. She was wearing a red cotton dress and red shoes and silk stockings. A white hat with a red top was found on the running board of the car. It had evidently been shot off during the gun battle."

The jury heard the six officers who had taken part in the slaying. They brought in a verdict that the two had died of gunshot wounds inflicted by officers acting in the line of duty.[7]

The combination furniture store and undertaking parlor was the scene of a mass riot. Crowds pushed and shoved to get a chance to view the mangled remains of the two desperadoes. "Doors of the store were torn off at their hinges by the mass of persons who flocked to the town by every known vehicle of transportation, including aeroplanes," the Austin *Daily Dispatch* reported.[8] The morbidly curious mob tore at one another in a ghoulish desire for souvenirs. Bits of Barrow's car were torn off and taken away.

"One woman," the *Daily Dispatch* continued, "was seen to snatch a piece of grey silk stocking which belonged to Bonnie and was dangling from the back seat of the car. The stocking was spotted with blood and one part was splotched with bits of brain."

"The shattered side and rear windows of the car were nearly intact when it was first towed into Arcadia, but not for long. Crowding, pushing, and almost fighting, the anxious people—estimated at nearly three thousand—jammed around the car and soon tore the glass from its holdings."[9]

Four or five bullets from the officers' guns had lodged in a tree across the road from the scene of the shootout. Men and women scrambled for them. They were finally removed by chopping out pieces of wood containing the spent bullets. One souvenir recovered at the scene was the shiny chromium-plated gas tank cap, which was snatched from the sedan while it was being moved to Arcadia. One man wanted to amputate Barrow's trigger finger, but the mob prevented him.[10]

"At five o'clock in the afternoon," the Dallas *Herald* reported, "it was impossible to purchase a cold drink in the town, and storekeepers and stand operators were calling frantically upon neighboring towns to send supplies to meet the unprecedented demand.

"Beer which sells at 15c a bottle during normal times, was sold for 25c. Cigarettes went up to 20c a package and it was almost impossible to get a sandwich, two slices of bread and a small piece of ham, at any price."

"Cars were parked so close together on the streets that, when an ambulance from Dallas arrived to get the body of Clyde Barrow, the driver had to call the local police to find a parking place."

"An amateur photographer, who had taken pictures of the car, bodies, guns and officers who participated in the killings was doing a land office business. Some out of town newspaper men, who didn't have their own photographers, were paying $5.00 each for them, and not doing a lot of kicking about the price."

"As soon as schools turned out Wednesday afternoon, there was a rush of children for the courthouse square, where the battered car had been taken."

"The roads leading into Arcadia were choked with traffic, and hundreds of cars were parked along the highway, the occupants walking for more than a mile to get to town."

"Sheriff Henderson Jordan had all his deputies and several state highway officers at work trying to handle the crowds."

"In the little room about eight feet by ten feet where the undertakers were trying to embalm the bodies several women and one man in the crowd were overcome by the heat and had to be carried out."

"At the leading hotel of the town, one was lucky to get a drink of water, and the negro porter was kept running from the well in the yard with a bucket to keep the cooler in the lobby filled with water."[11]

When the Parker family learned of Bonnie's death, her brother, Buster, drove to Arcadia. Enraged at the slaying, he paced up and down beside her body, cursing her slayers. "A low down stool pigeon put them on the spot," he cried to whoever would listen, "otherwise no ten laws would face them."[12]

"I couldn't help thinking about the reward of these two," Simmons recalled. "I wondered if it might have turned out otherwise for both of them if they had had better childhood surroundings and training. Clyde and Bonnie were put on the spot. I made no apology for that."

Speaking of the reactions of their families, he continued: "The criminals' mothers had plenty of things to say, all of which I have long since excused. Fathers sometimes forsake their offspring when they get into trouble; mothers never do. As Clyde and Bonnie had dealt, so had they received. As they had sowed, so also had they reaped."[13]

23

"I feel a damn sight better driving around at night."

The news made headlines across the country. Hamer was applauded not only in the press, but also on the floor of Congress. The Speaker set aside time for the Congressmen to praise Hamer. Congressman Robert Kleberg from Texas said:

"Mr. Speaker, my purpose in taking this fragment of time is to congratulate the Nation and the State of Texas and Captain Frank Hamer, ex-Texas Ranger, and other officers who participated, for the work done in ridding their State of its public enemy No. 1, Mr. Clyde Barrow."

"I feel, generally speaking, that in matters of this sort the attention of this country should be directed to the fact efficiency still exists in the ranks of those who have to do with the enforcement of our country's laws. The State of Texas, of course, has been equipped for many years with a constabulary which, in my opinion, has done great service to the nation without reference to the infinite good they have done the people of the State of Texas in the invaluable service they have rendered from the time of their creation as an official group for the protection of the peace and dignity of my great state."

"I do not want to take too much time this morning, but while Mr. Frank Hamer was not at the time of the apprehension of Clyde Barrow and his consort a member of the Texas Rangers, he had served as a Ranger for twenty-five years, and it goes without saying that he knew his business. I think it would be well for the country generally to find out just exactly how the problem of apprehending this man was worked out in the brief period of time after Captain Hamer took his trail. I would suggest to the Department of Justice that they might learn something of benefit were they to look into the actual machinations and development of the plan which finally brought this career of crime to an end."[1]

A special resolution thanking Hamer for his "work in behalf of law and order" was passed by Congress, and the Texas Legislature passed a similar tribute.[2]

The Austin newspaper ran a front page headline in three-inch letters proclaiming: "HAMER-GAULT HERO DAY IS SET!" Citizens planned a testimonial dinner for Hamer and Gault, to be held on Monday, May 28. A barbecue, an informal dinner, and speeches were planned. The governor, the police force, the highway patrol, the Ranger force, and state officials, as well as the local citizenry would be in attendance.[3]

A poem was even composed to commemorate the brave actions of the officers. It ended:

> May it go down in history,
> That we dedicate Hamer Day,
> And Manny Gault received his honor
> For the part he played in May.[4]

When Hamer was informed of the plans, he declined to attend. The unassuming Ranger stated, "I have a date with a man downtown that evening." This was the remark he always made to his family when he had to go out on a case. The testimonial was cancelled.[5]

Thousands of letters and telegrams flowed in. Associated Press offered Hamer cash for a firsthand account of the gun battle, but Hamer refused.[6] Dud Barker, the sheriff who had first recommended Hamer for the Rangers nearly thirty years previously wrote: "I want you to know that I am still for you, and I am proud of you and your good work. I tell them all that you are the best officer that ever wore a gun."[7]

A man sent a telegram that stated simply: "I feel a damn sight safer driving around at night now thanks to you."[8]

Just before sunset on May 25, Barrow was buried on a chalky West Dallas hillside near his boyhood home. Hamer attended, but turned away in disgust as souvenir seekers snatched roses, gladiolas, and peonies from the grave, while Barrow's aged mother was led away weeping.[9]

Bonnie indicated in one of her poems that she wanted to be buried beside Clyde, but her mother refused. "Now that she's dead, she's all mine," she said. "I don't want her buried with Clyde. He had her while she was alive."[10] On Saturday, May 26, Bonnie was buried in a steel casket at the West Dallas Fishtrap Cemetery.[11]

On the day that Bonnie and Clyde met their death, Bonnie's sister, Billie Parker Mace, and Hamilton's brother, Floyd, were on trial in Fort Worth for the killing of the two highway patrolmen at Grapevine. When Hamer returned to Austin after the gun battle, he went to aid Bonnie's sister. "I know just as surely that Clyde Barrow and Bonnie Parker did it," he told the court and the press, "as I knew surely where they would be last Wednesday morning. They talked to people about the killing and described it. Just because Floyd is related to Ray Hamilton and Mrs. Mace to Bonnie Parker is no reason to fasten this on them. I know they did not do it."[12]

The big lawman went out of his way to help clear Billie and Floyd, and his testimony, together with the evidence of the fingerprints on the whiskey bottle, resulted in their being cleared of the murder.

Hamilton, about this time, robbed the First National Bank of Lewisville, Texas, and fled to Grayson County, where he was arrested. He was sent to Huntsville on a ninety-nine year sentence, but escaped once more and began robbing banks again. He was finally recaptured in Fort Worth and sent to the electric chair on May 10, 1935.[13]

For several years, the Texas legislature had wanted to abolish the Texas Rangers and merge the force with the highway patrol. Hamer's tracking of Bonnie and Clyde stopped the movement, and quite possibly saved the Texas Rangers. "Texas did so much better a job of winding up the Clyde Barrow situation than a renowned State Police force did the Lindberg baby kidnapping, and in the midwestern Dillinger hunt," said one newspaper editorial, "that the Ranger service has vindicated itself and gained new laurels. Frank Hamer, steeped in the tradition of the Ranger Service, and Manny Gault, a typical Ranger, showed the nation the kind of officers it takes to deal with the rabid criminal. Such a surge of admiration and enthusiasm for the Ranger service resulted from Hamer and

Gault's achievement this week that proposing to destroy the identity of the Texan Rangers now probably would be hooted down."[14]

Considerable publicity was given to the possibility that Hamer would be put on the trail of John Dillinger. W. W. Sterling, former Adjutant General of Texas, corresponded with J. Edgar Hoover about the possibility. So much publicity was aroused, however, that Hamer refused to consider the job. He felt that he had become such a public figure that it would be impossible for him to work anonymously. People hinted that Hamer had already helped the Justice Department on the case, he having learned that Dillinger had plastic surgery on his face earlier in the year in Louisiana.[15]

The stolen guns and the ammunition from the fugitives' car were awarded to Hamer by the authorities. Because collectors would have paid a good deal of money for them, both Bonnie and Clyde's families tried to get them back. On July 28, 1934, Clyde's mother wrote to Hamer:

"Mr. Hamer, we have been told here by Sheriff Smoot Shmid in Dallas that you have in your possession some guns that were in the car at the time you and the officers killed my boy Clyde. Now Mr. Hamer, I do hope you will be kindly enough to give me those guns as you know you have no right to try and keep those guns. I feel you should think you have caused me enough grief and hardships without trying to cause me more trouble now. I have been told you got out of the car three pistols and one saw off shotgun. Now I do know that my boy did buy most of the guns he had so I don't see why you should not return the ones you have to me. You don't never want to forget my boy was never tried in no court for murder and no one is guilty until proven guilty by some court so I hope you will answer this letter and also return the guns I am asking for. (signed) Mrs. C. H. Barrow."[16]

On October 16, Parker's mother wrote Hamer:

"From an article which appeared in the Dallas *Times Herald* under dateline September 27, 1934 from Austin, I have information that you are now in possession of and evidently laying claim to a certain shot-gun, being a 20 gauge shot-gun which bears the name of my deceased daughter; you have having registered such firearm in your name in the Internal Revenue Collector's office, evidently at Austin."

"You are advised that as the mother of Bonnie Parker it is my desire and I at this time make claim to the right of possession of such guns as the personal property of my deceased daughter. Other officers, namely the Sheriff from Shreveport, Louisiana, has already turned over to me other personal property which belonged to my daughter."

"So long as I am planning to leave Dallas for rather an extended length of time I am turning this matter over to my attorney . . . and would appreciate it if you would ship the gun to him, charges collect for shipment, or should you care to communicate with me kindly do so through his office as I have today talked to him regarding this matter and my rights thereunder. Yours truly, (signed) Mrs. E. Parker."[17]

Their efforts were in vain. Hamer registered the sawed-off shotguns and Brownings and stored them upstairs at his home. So long as he lived, he never accepted any of the monetary offers to tell the story of the capture, although magazines, and the radio and motion picture industries, made numerous offers. He maintained, to the end of his life, that the story of his career and the royalties it would bring would be part of the inheritance he would pass to his family.[18]

Simmons recalled that, on the night of Bonnie and Clyde's deaths, "Hamer and I were in our hotel room . . . when the telephone rang at midnight. It was New York, calling Captain Frank Hamer. Hamer answered and what I heard was something like this: 'Yes, this is Hamer—Yes—National Broadcasting Company?—How's that?—A thousand dollars for a few minutes' talk over the radio?—Hell, no!—I won't do it.—What do you think I am?—Hell, no!' He slammed the receiver on the hook, cussing a blue streak and mad as a hornet. I know men who would have leaped at the publicity, to say nothing of the thousand dollars. But not Hamer."[19]

A score of motion picture idols visited Hamer during the following years to attempt him into releasing rights to the story. He remained steadfast in his refusal.[20] "I am not a wealthy man," he would say, "but my family will be able to support itself on royalties from the story of my career after I die, and I want them to benefit from it then."[21]

Near the end of 1934, a man obtained the mutilated car belonging to Bonnie and Clyde. He put together a tent show with gory slides of Bonnie and Clyde, "Pretty Boy" Floyd, John Dillinger, and other criminals. The man used Hamer's name, capitalizing heavily on the part Hamer had played in the capture.

When the show arrived in Austin, Hamer heard the man barking his show—describing in morbid detail the splitting of Clyde's skull and the bullets in Bonnie's body. Hamer listened, until he had heard enough. He jumped up on the platform and said, "I'm Frank Hamer."

The man resisted, and Hamer slapped him soundly across the face. "Don't ever use my name again in public," he threatened. Hamer stalked off the stage, and the showman was not heard from again until after Hamer's death some twenty years later.[22]

Two months after the gun battle, Sheriff Henderson Jordan went to Huntsville to talk with Simmons about a pardon or parole for Methvin. As far as the public was concerned, Methvin was still at large. But on orders from Sheriff Jordan, Methvin was staying close to his home in Louisiana and was not being bothered by law enforcement officers. The sheriff told Simmons that the Methvins were insisting on "something being done immediately," and recommended that executive clemency be obtained. Simmons assured the sheriff that it could be taken care of and contacted Hamer. On August 11, 1934, Hamer and Simmons talked the matter over and sent a letter to Governor Miriam Ferguson, stating:

"You recall that on January 16, 1934, Clyde Barrow and associates raided the Eastham Prison Farm and delivered from there Raymond Hamilton, Joe Palmer, Hilton Bybee, Henry Methvin, and other prisoners. At that time Clyde Barrow was on parole granted by Governor Sterling, but said parole had been revoked and the officers in the entire southwest were endeavoring to capture Clyde Barrow."

"With your approval, I employed Mr. Frank Hamer on February 10 as Special Escape Investigator for the Texas Prison System. After several months work, it developed that perhaps Barrow and associates could be trapped with the assistance of relatives and friends of Henry Methvin, who lived in Louisiana."

"Through Henderson Jordan of Arcadia, and with close friends of the Methvin family whereby, if aid was given to the prison officials, it was agreed that if Clyde Barrow were captured or killed clemency could be obtained for Henry Methvin; and, after conference with Governor Jim Ferguson and yourself, my letter of April 24, 1934, to Captain Hamer was delivered to the friends of Henry Methvin, this letter being submitted to you, same meeting with your approval."

"It was through this arrangement that Clyde Barrow and Bonnie Parker were taken and, therefore, Captain Hamer and myself are now recommending and asking that pardon be granted to Henry Methvin in order that the contract made by us be carried out. In my judgment, Henry Methvin knew nothing of this arrangement, and had nothing to do with the same, but same was made by his father and friends, in order to save the life of same Henry Methvin. We believe that the extermination of Clyde Barrow was entirely justifiable, as he had shown an utter disregard for the lives of citizens and peace officers of the country, and there is no question that he murdered many good peace officers ruthlessly without any cause and that he had an utter disregard for human life. Therefore, as stated, we recommend to you and ask that full pardon be granted to Henry Methvin."

"This, of course, in no way has anything to do with any other crimes committed by Henry Methvin, as in my letter I made the statement that this refers only to his crime that he is now serving on."[23]

The Fergusons called Hamer and Simmons to the governor's office and agreed to Methvin's pardon for giving "valuable information that led to the apprehension and capture of one Clyde Barrow and one Bonnie Parker."[24]

Shortly thereafter, Methvin wrote to Hamer, stating: "I received my pardon and thank you very much for what you have done for me. Mr. Hamer, I am in need of work and if you know of any place you can get me a job I would appreciate it very much."[25]

Hamer looked for a job for Methvin, but Oklahoma officers arrested the young man and took him to Oklahoma to stand trial for crimes committed there. He was convicted and given the death sentence. It was later commuted to life imprisonment, and Methvin was finally pardoned by the governor of Oklahoma. Hamer helped the young man find employment and heard from him from time to time.

24

"The next thing I saw was the bottom of the man's feet."

In 1935, Hamer was asked to help avert a port strike in Houston, and he accepted. He drove to Houston and went to the docks, where the striking workers had formed a mob. Strikes meant sabotage in those days, and this particular mob, made up of tough stevedores and dock workers, was a rough one.

Hamer surveyed the group from a distance of fifty yards. Alone, he slowly walked up to them. Some of the members were throwing bricks; others waved clubs. They paused as the big man approached. Hamer strode up to the largest man in the front ranks, and with his open hand, knocked him senseless to the ground.

"I'm Frank Hamer," he said. "This strike is over!"

The stunned gang looked at Hamer, who returned their stares coolly. One of the men recognized the ex-Ranger captain as the man who had "taken care" of Bonnie and Clyde, and this information quickly spread. Hamer waited, ready for anything that might happen. Finally, one man turned and left, followed by another, then another. In a short while, the rest of the mob melted away and the strike was temporarily ended.[1]

Port Director J. Russell Wait was so impressed that he asked Hamer to stay on. During the past two years, strikes and sabotage had almost disabled the Port of Houston, and they seemed to be increasing. State and municipal authorities arranged for Hamer to lead a special force of some twenty ex-Rangers and ex-sheriffs to prevent sabotage, looting, and illegal strike activities in the port city.[2]

Throughout 1935 and the early part of 1936, Hamer and his twenty associates worked to protect the port. There was an occasional mob to disperse, but dynamiters were the biggest problem. By the middle of 1936, however, the port was operating peacefully, and Hamer told the commissioner that he felt his job had been done. Wait wrote to Hamer:

"At the time you entered the employment of this Commission, there was a real crisis confronting the port, and it was interesting to see the wonderful effect which your presence had on the disorganization which confronted the port interests as a result of a strike which was a follow-up of a strike in 1934, which was handled so inefficiently as to seriously hurt the port, and most people felt that the port was in for a bad period as a result of the experiences gained in the 1934 strike."

"The most satisfactory thing that I had noticed in my close contact with you was the high quality of your associates, the fidelity with which they followed your instructions, the loyalty to you personally and the fact that not one single incident of insubordination or difficulty of any kind has characterized your handling of a very dangerous and disagreeable situation."

"It is a pleasure on my part to voluntarily advise you that I have watched very carefully the method which you have used in knowing what was going on, and your method in following up all such information in so thorough a manner as to forestall dangerous activities on the part of dangerous people."

"It is my hope that in the future our paths will cross again, because I must frankly state that I have learned to admire your methods very much, and I look for you to be high in the law enforcement circles of this fine State before many years."[3]

With his small force, Hamer stayed on in Houston and joined forces with Houston ex-police chief Roy T. Rogers to open a security guard association. For the next thirteen years, Hamer and Rogers protected oil fields, refineries, chemical plants, docks, and shipping firms from sabotage and illegal striking activities. The firm grew to employ several hundred men and covered the entire Gulf Coast area.

In 1939, another major strike broke out at the Port of Houston. A picket line was formed, and anyone who crossed it, received a severe beating. Hamer and Rogers were called in to provide safety for those who wanted to cross the line. Professional thugs—men who had made a career of striking and intimidating those who refused to strike—had been called in from New Jersey and New York. Hamer and Rogers drove up to the line and demanded to be let through. One of the imported "dock wallopers" let loose a violent stream of curse words at Hamer. Hamer looked up at the man, cupped his hand behind his ear, and said:

"What's that you said? I'm a little hard of hearing."

The man repeated his invectives, adding a few more that were raw even for the strikers. Everyone gathered close to the car to hear what Hamer had to say.

"Well, I'm sorry, sir," Hamer answered. "I just can't seem to hear you in here." Then he opened the car door and stepped out.

Rogers later recounted the end of the story: "The next thing I saw was the bottom of the man's feet going up in the air. When the man hit the ground, all those tough pickets started applauding, as the man had no cause to be that foul-mouthed. We drove on through, down to the office, and I looked back, noticing that the pickets weren't even picking up the dock walloper. We came back out about twenty minutes later and the man was still lying there in the middle of the drive."[4]

No matter where he went, Hamer was constantly being hounded for the "inside story" on the Barrow–Parker case. In 1939, Hamer's son, Frank, Jr., was working in Houston as a special officer for an oil company. One day, wearing his pistol and a short jacket, he walked into a barber shop in West University Place. While he was getting his hair cut, the barber began talking about law enforcement.

"You know, I've got a close friend who killed Clyde Barrow and Bonnie Parker," the barber commented.

"Is that so?" Frank, Jr., replied, raising his eyebrows.

"Yes, I was with him on the case," the barber continued. "Very few people knew he was after them, but he told me and I helped him out. If it hadn't been for me, he would be a nobody now. His name is Frank Hamer. Do you know him?"

"Slightly," young Frank answered.

The barber droned on about his close friendship with the Hamer family, and the other barbers and customers listened with rapt attention.

As Frank, Jr., got out of the chair, the barber asked, "By the way, sonny, what's your name?"

"Frank Hamer, Jr.," he answered, looking the barber straight in the eye.

"If I had had a camera with me that day," Frank, Jr., later reminisced, "I'd have gotten a prize-winning shot. I just can't describe the look on that barber's face when his fellow barbers and the customers broke into peals of laughter. Later, I learned that the barber had been a bailiff down around Pasadena, and had once met

Dad. I would say that I have met a thousand people who have said that they knew all about Dad's being on the Barrow case long before it made the newspapers. Besides Mother, Billy, and me, there weren't five other people who really knew about it. I hate to think about the hurrahing that barber must have taken from the other barbers from then on."[5]

On one occasion, a reporter got Hamer to open up about his past.

"How many men have you killed?" the reporter asked.

"I won't talk about that," Hamer replied,

"They say you've killed twenty-three men, not counting Mexicans."

"I won't discuss it. All my killings were in the line of duty. It was an unpleasant duty," Hamer admitted.

"How many gun fights have you been in?" the reporter asked.

"I don't mind telling you that," Hamer said. "I have been in fifty-two of them."

The reporter persisted. "How many times have you been shot?"

"I've been wounded by bullets twenty-three times," Hamer answered. "Several of those bullets are in me yet. I'd rather have them in than to go through the trouble of having them cut out. I don't know how many times I've been hit by shotgun blasts."

The newspaperman continued to press Hamer for details, but he would only admit, "I've been ambushed four different times and shot down, left for dead, twice. I was on crutches for almost a year from wounds given me by men who were paid to kill me."

"Did you ever find out who they were?"

"I did."

"And you had them arrested," the reporter asked.

"No, they were never arrested," Hamer said with a grunt. And that ended the interview.[6]

25

"That's the only man I ever killed . . ."

When World War II broke out in 1939, Hamer wrote to the King of England offering to bring fifty ex-Rangers to England to be used for coastal protection and to prevent sabotage that was so prevalent. Enemy saboteurs were being parachuted into England at night, and Hamer felt that his Rangers could be used to prevent this. On September 5, 1939, he received the following telegram:

"The King greatly appreciates your offer. Please apply British Embassy, Washington."[1]

Hamer began making arrangements, when the U.S. government, eager to protect its neutral status, nipped the plan in the bud.[2] At the same time, however, the United States stepped up its production of war material, and Houston refineries and chemical plants increased their production to the maximum. More extensive protection systems were required, and Hamer and his men found that they had more than they could handle on the home front.

In 1941, when the United States declared war, both of Hamer's sons volunteered for the Marines, although both had wives and children and could have remained at home. Frank, Jr., became a Marine pilot, and Billy joined the Marine infantry. Just before Christmas in 1944, Billy sent Gladys the following poem as a Christmas present:

Merry Xmas, Mom,
I may be thousands of miles away,
But I am thinking of you today.
I hope you have lots of happiness and good cheer,
And remember that I love you dear.
All my love,
Billy[3]

For the next five months, while Billy was in the South Pacific, the Hamers received no other word from him. In May 1945, when the war was almost ended, the dreaded telegram from the War Department arrived. Billy had been killed in the storming of Iwo Jima.[4]

Hamer and Rogers were in Houston at the time, and Rogers recalls: "We were sleeping in a room up on about the fifteenth floor of the Rice Hotel when he received the call from his wife telling about Billy. Cap told me what had happened, then pulled a chair over to the window and opened it, then looked out. He sat there for almost two days and nights, it seemed, and must have smoked a half carton of cigarettes. He didn't eat, or drink, or sleep during the whole time, and wouldn't even answer the telephone."[5]

It was 1946 before Billy's body was brought home. He was given a hero's burial with full military honors. Ranger Chaplain P. B. Hill led the ceremonies.

Billy's death was the severest blow of Hamer's life. For some time, it seemed that he had given up. But he was able to lose himself in his work, and the Hamer–Rogers firm had more than enough work.

In 1948, Hamer participated in his last major activity as a Texas Ranger. In the 1948 election, the voting returns in Jim Wells County were contested, and Governor Coke Stevenson asked Captain Hamer to accompany him and two former FBI agents to inspect the ballots in Ballot Box 13, held in a bank vault in Jim Wells County.

The bank was surrounded by armed men who refused to allow anyone to enter. Hamer and Governor Stevenson approached the bank on foot, and Hamer stepped up to the guards.

"Git!" he told the first group, most of whom knew him and his reputation as a peace officer. They moved away.

Hamer and the governor then went up to the bank door, which was guarded by another group of armed men. "Fall back!" Hamer ordered. They did.

The governor and his party were allowed to enter the bank and to inspect the ballots briefly. A political controversy of no small significance raged for some time thereafter.[6]

In the spring of 1940, Hamer took a train trip to California with his old friend, Paul Hochuli. The train passed through Hamer's old stomping grounds in West Texas, and Hamer reminisced about his early days as a Texas Ranger. One story he told Hochuli was about a Ranger he had known just before World War I.

"He was a God-fearing man," Hamer related, "and observed the Sabbath. He wouldn't even read his mail on Sunday. I remember one Sunday a gunman insulted him, but he let the insult go. The next day, however, he buckled on his guns, looked up the gunman, and killed him."[7]

In Hollywood, Hochuli and Hamer met Roy Rogers, the cowboy star, and visited in his Hollywood home. Hamer had a fine time viewing Rogers' gun collection, and Rogers pressed Hamer to allow his story to be told. But Hamer refused, saying, "Wait'll I'm dead." Rogers had a photographer take a picture of them together, and asked Hamer for his autograph.[8]

Later in the same year, the New York Yankees played an exhibition baseball game in Houston. Captain Hamer and a friend were sitting in a restaurant, when Lefty Gomez and Joe DiMaggio walked in with a crowd of men. Someone pointed out Hamer to the ballplayers and told them that he was a famous Texas Ranger captain. DiMaggio walked over to Hamer's table and introduced himself. He asked Hamer for his autograph, and the captain gave it to him and asked him to sit down. The two struck up a conversation, and DiMaggio asked him. "Captain Hamer, they tell me you've killed between forty-five and fifty men."

"No, no," Hamer replied with a smile. "But now that I think of it, there was one time when we were out moving some cattle across New Mexico, and we got caught in a snowstorm. I was sleeping with an old boy, and when it came time for me to get up and go on night herd, I failed to pull the saddle blanket back up over him, and he froze to death. Near as I can recollect, that's the only man I've ever killed in my whole life."

DiMaggio looked at Hamer in astonishment, then caught the twinkle in his eye. DiMaggio dropped to the floor, convulsed with laughter. "If you want to talk to me anymore," he said, "I'm down here."[9]

The humid Houston climate caused Hamer's wounds to bother him. Late in 1949, when Hamer was sixty-five, he sold out to his partner, Roberts, and moved back to Austin. Life was more leisurely there, and Hamer gradually eased into permanent retirement. He still received letters and visitors from Hollywood, many trying to obtain permission to use his life story in a movie or in a television serial.

But Hamer was enjoying retirement. Frank, Jr., served as a Ranger on the personal staff of Governor Allan Shivers, and as a pilot and game warden for the Texas Parks and Wildlife Commission. He lived with his family in nearby San Marcos, and the two Hamer families were able to visit together often.

Hamer's last years in Austin were pleasant ones. He loved to gather with old friends and reminisce about the "good old days." Walter Webb, J. Frank Dobie, Bill Sterling, Bill Kuykendall, and scores of other would visit with the Hamers, play a little pitch or no-ante poker, and chew the fat.

One time when Dobie and Hamer were relating tales to each other, they got on to the subject of jack rabbits. They were remarking on how the jack rabbit is more agile than is generally realized. Dobie later wrote an article about his conversation with Hamer:

"'I was riding along one day on the Staked Plains.' Captain Frank Hamer of Texas Ranger fame related, 'when I saw a jack rabbit running full tilt parallel to my course. I expected to see a coyote after him, but when I turned in the saddle to look back I saw an eagle flying. He was overtaking the rabbit, dipping lower and lower, his talons extended."

"Just when the jack rabbit looked to be a goner, he stopped and squatted low on the ground. Then the eagle began to circle over him swooping closer and closer until he zoomed groundward. I could see the whole thing, neither animal seeming conscious of my existence. Old Jack had his ears laid back flat and waited until the eagle was right at him. Then he sprang about six feet straight up, his feet fanning the air. The eagle passed under him."

"When he hit the ground he was running like an antelope. He made a full three hundred yards before the jack rabbit made it to a little catclaw bush, where he had protection from air attack and was safe."[10]

In 1953 Captain Hamer suffered a heat stroke and spent the majority of the next two years indoors. On Sunday, July 10, 1955, at the age of seventy-one, Hamer died peacefully in his sleep.

Ranger Chaplain P. B. Hill led the ceremonies at his funeral. Pallbearers included old friends such as W. W. Sterling, Lee Simmons, Tom Hickman, Charlie Miller, A. W. Billingsley, Bill Kuykendall, and others.

Hill, who had given services for so many other Rangers and law officers, spoke about Hamer: "My friends, here before us lies the remains of one of the greatest men I ever knew . . . a man who feared Almighty God but never feared the face of any man. . . . You know, many people don't understand law officers—I think probably most people don't understand them. I wonder if we really appreciate what these men do. How poorly they're paid, what risks they run. Tonight we sleep soundly and well, our lives, our property well protected—it's not because of some law that has been passed, but because men in the cities and in the country— Rangers, sheriffs, deputies, and constables—are quietly moving here and there, and the criminals know it. We sleep soundly because of these men."

"I remember one time when Hamer was in a shoe store, and a woman came in and ordered a large number of children's shoes. Hamer asked, 'Who is that woman?' The salesman answered that she was buying the shoes for an orphanage. 'I want you to do me a favor,' Hamer told the man. 'Put the shoes on my bill, and send them on out there now.' Very few people knew that about Frank."

"Another time, Frank was given a fairly large reward check, but he didn't have any use for it. He went to a boy who had given him a tip on the case, endorsed the check, and said, 'Son, I want you to use the check to go to school.' Only when the books of God are open will folks really know all the secret things that Frank Hamer did, for charity, for the deserving, and for the undeserving as well."

"Frank was one of the most colorful officers that Texas has ever produced. . . . J. Edgar Hoover said one time that Frank Hamer was one of the greatest law officers in American history. He was the personification of those qualities that make a great officer, the qualities that make Texas Rangers famous."[11]

An era had ended.

"Frank Hamer's service," Walter Prescott Webb said, "covered that period of transition in Texas from frontier simplicity and directness to modern complexity. . . . From the study of boot-heel prints and horse tracks, Frank Hamer graduated to the Bertillon system and hotel registers. Few men have been able to make this transition from one school of crime to another so entirely different."[12]

To Webb the historian, he ranked with Jack Hays and Ben McCulloch, as one of the three "most fearless men in Western history."[13] To the newspapermen he was that "giant of a man, moon-faced, always in boots, and as talkative as an oyster."[14] To Texas governors he was "the best, most honest, and most efficient peace officer Texas has ever known"[15] To the world he was a legend—a legend based on facts that did not need embellishment or exaggeration.

"I last saw him" one of his friends recalled, "on a mountain road, west of Austin, his home. His right hand was gripped on the steering wheel of the car which he was driving at a slack pace. His left hand clutched a pistol whose blasts kept plowing up spurts of dirt under a rock a little piece ahead."

"Past 65 Frank Hamer must have been then. But not once did his aim falter."

"Not once did the gun miss. Not once did the rock stop bobbing and turning. . . . "

"It will be a long time," someone else wrote after his death, "before another officer as picturesque and as blunt, as stubborn and as fearless, will pass this way again."[15]

ANNOTATION

Chapter 1

1. Frank A. Hamer, Jr., interview with H. Gordon Frost and John H. Jenkins, Austin, Texas, June 13, 1967; Harrison Hamer, interview with John H. Jenkins, Giddings, Texas, July 25, 1967. Typescripts in Hamer family papers.
2. Mrs. Gladys Hamer, interview with John H. Jenkins and H. Gordon Frost, Austin, Texas, April 14, 1967. Copy in Hamer family papers.
3. Birth certificate, Hamer family papers.
4. Gladys Hamer interview, op. cit.
5. Dobie, *Guide to Life and Literature of the Southwest*, 58.
6. Webb, *The Texas Rangers*, 521.
7. Ibid., 521–522.

Chapter 2

1. Harrison Hamer interview, op. cit.
2. Bill Kuykendall and Marshall Kuykendall, interview with H. Gordon Frost, Kyle, Texas, July 12, 1967. Copy in Hamer family papers.
3. Ibid.
4. Harrison Hamer interview, op cit.
5. P. B. Hill, funeral eulogy to Capt. Frank Hamer, Austin, 1955. Copy in Hamer family papers.

Chapter 3

1. Frank Hamer, Jr., interview, op. cit.
2. Webb and Carroll (eds.), *The Handbook of Texas*, I, 953.
3. Webb, *Rangers*, op. cit., 530–531.
4. Frank A. Hamer, Jr., interview, op. cit.
5. Gladys Hamer interview, op. cit.; Frank A. Hamer Jr., interview, op. cit.; Webb, *Rangers*, op. cit., 524.

Chapter 4

1. Webb, *Rangers*, op. cit., 522–523.
2. Ibid., 525–526.
3. Gladys Hamer interview, op. cit. Webb, *Rangers*, op. cit., 525–526.

Chapter 5

1. D. S. Barker to the Adjutant General of Texas, March 11, 1906, original in Texas Ranger Archives, Austin.

2. Enlistment certificate. Hamer family papers.
3. Hunter and Rose, *The Album of Gunfighters*, 100.
4. Harrison Hamer interview, op. cit.: Frank A. Hamer, Jr., interview, op. cit.
5. Hunter and Rose, op. cit., 100.
6. Del Rio *Times*, September 29, 1906.
7. Navasota *Examiner-Review*, December 3, 1908.
8. Frank A. Hamer, Jr., interview, op. cit.
9. Ibid; Kinney, "Frank Hamer, Texas Ranger," 83.
10. Webb, *Rangers*, op. cit., 527.
11. Navasota *Examiner-Review*, July 21, 1910.
12. Webb, *Rangers*, op. cit., 527.
13. Sterling, *Trails and Trials of a Texas Ranger*, 421.
14. Ibid.
15. Ibid.
16. Navasota *Examiner-Review*, July 28, 1910.
17. Ibid, January 14, 1909.
18. Clipping, Hamer family scrapbooks.
19. Navasota *Examiner-Review*, August 2, 1910.
20. Webb, *Rangers*, op. cit., 527.
21. Frank A. Hamer, Jr., op. cit.
22. Clipping, Hamer family scrapbooks.

Chapter 6

1. Clipping, Hamer family papers.
2. Houston *Press*, clipping, Hamer family papers.
3. Ibid., clipping, Hamer family papers.
4. Houston *Chronicle*, clipping, Hamer family papers.
5. Clippings, Ibid.
6. Clipping, Ibid.
7. Gladys Hamer, interview, op. cit.
8. Webb, *Rangers*, op. cit., 528.
9. Bill and Marshall Kuykendall interview, op. cit.

Chapter 7

1. Webb, *Rangers*, op. cit., 485.
2. Copy in Hamer family papers.
3. Webb, *Rangers*, op. cit., 484.
4. Ibid., 483.
5. Enlistment form, Hamer family papers.

6. Lea, *The King Ranch,* 583–584.

7. Bob Snow, interview with H. Gordon Frost, Ingram, Texas, June 14, 1967.

8. Ibid.

9. Ibid; Frank A. Hamer, Jr., op. cit.

10. Bob Snow interview, op. cit.; Frank A. Hamer, Jr., interview, op. cit.

Chapter 8

1. El Paso *Times,* October 14, 1915.

2. Webb, *Rangers,* op. cit., 531–532.

3. Clipping, Hamer family papers.

4. Webb, *Rangers,* op. cit., 532.

5. Bob Snow interview, op. cit.

Chapter 9

1. Capt. John H. Rogers to the Texas Cattle Raisers Association, June 2, 1916, signed carbon in Hamer family papers.

2. Gladys Hamer interview, op. cit.

3. Gladys Hamer to H. Gordon Frost, July 17, 1967.

4. Kinney, op. cit., 84.

5. Ibid; Frank A. Hamer, Jr., interview, op. cit.; Harrison Hamer interview, op. cit.

6. Hamer family papers.

7. Harrison Hamer interview, op. cit.

8. Frank A. Hamer, Jr., interview, op. cit.

9. Harrison Hamer interview, op. cit.

10. Capt. Frank Hamer to Sam H. Hill, December 1, 1932, copy in Hamer family papers.

11. Harrison Hamer interview, op. cit.

12. Ibid.

13. Capt. Frank Hamer to Sam H. Hill, December 1, 1932, copy in Hamer family papers.

14. Ibid.

15. Harrison Hamer interview, op cit.; Gladys Hamer interview, op. cit.

16. Capt. Frank Hamer to Sam H. Hill, December 1, 1932, copy in Hamer family papers.

17. Ibid.

18. Harrison Hamer interview, *op. cit.*

19. Ibid; Gladys Hamer interview, op. cit.; Frank A. Hamer, Jr., interview, op. cit.

20. Ibid; Kinney, op. cit., 84.

21. Kinney, op. cit., 84.

Chapter 10

1. Harrison Hamer interview, op. cit.
2. Ibid; Gladys Hamer interview, op. cit.; Frank A. Hamer, Jr., interview, op. cit.
3. Kinney, op. cit., 82.
4. Dallas *News*, July 12, 1955.
5. Kinney, op. cit., 83.
6. Ibid.
7. Reenlistment papers, Texas Ranger Archives, Austin.
8. El Paso *Times*, September 8, 1917.
9. Owen P. White, *Them Was the Days*, 112–113.
10. Webb, *Rangers*, op. cit., 529.
11. Frank A. Hamer, Jr., interview, op. cit.
12. Webb, *Rangers*, op. cit., 529–530.
13. Bob Snow interview, op. cit.; Frank A. Hamer, Jr., interview, op. cit.; Roy T. Rogers, interview with H. Gordon Frost, Houston, June 10, 1967, copy in Hamer family papers.

Chapter 11

1. Webb, *Rangers*, op. cit., 513.
2. Sterling, op. cit., 93.
3. Frank A. Hamer, Jr., interview, op. cit.
4. Clipping, Hamer family papers.
5. Ibid.
6. Ibid.
7. Frank A. Hamer, Jr., interview, op. cit.
8. Clipping, Hamer family papers.
9. Reenlistment papers, Texas Ranger Archives, Austin.
10. Clipping, Hamer family papers.
11. Ibid.
12. Gladys Hamer interview, op. cit.; Frank Hamer to Texas Adjutant General, telegram, Texas Ranger Archives, Austin.

Chapter 12

1. Harrison Hamer interview, op. cit.
2. Clipping, Hamer family papers.
3. Ibid.
4. Frank A. Hamer, Jr., interview, op. cit.
5. Ibid.
6. Clipping, Hamer family papers.

7. Webb, *Rangers*, op. cit., 530.
8. Pat M. Neff, *The Battles of Peace*, 141–142.
9. Clipping, Hamer family papers.
10. Gen. Jacob F. Wolters to Gov. Pat M. Neff, copy in Hamer family papers.
11. Ibid.
12. Ibid.
13. Ibid.
14. Austin *American*, February 2, 1922.
15. Wolters to Neff, op. cit.
16. Ibid.
17. Gov. Pat M. Neff to Capt. Frank Hamer, March 6, 1922, original in Hamer family papers.
18. Wolters to Neff, op. cit.

Chapter 13

1. Frank A. Hamer, Jr., interview, op. cit.
2. Kinney, op. cit., 83.
3. Webb, *Rangers*, op. cit., 524.
4. Ibid.
5. Frank A. Hamer, Jr., interview, op. cit.
6. Clipping, Hamer family scrapbooks.
7. Gladys Hamer interview, op. cit.
8. Clipping, Hamer family papers.
9. Ibid.
10. Kinney, op. cit., 86.
11. Gladys Hamer interview, op. cit.; Frank A. Hamer, Jr., interview, op. cit.
12. Ibid.
13. Ibid.

Chapter 14

1. Austin *American*, June 3, 1925.
2. Gov. Pat M. Neff to Capt. Frank Hamer, July 12, 1925, original in Hamer family papers.
3. Bill and Marshall Kuykendall interview, op. cit.
4. Clipping, Hamer family papers.
5. Sterling, op. cit., 130.
6. Ibid, 133.
7. Portland *Oregonian*, February 2, 1926.
8. Deposition, Hamer family papers.
9. R. D. "Boss" Thorp, interview with H. Gordon Frost, Austin, June 13, 1967.

Chapter 15

1. Webb, *Rangers*, op. cit., 531.
2. Ibid.
3. Bill and Marshall Kuykendall interview, op. cit.
4. Clipping, Hamer family scrapbooks.
5. Eugene Manlove Rhodes to Walter P. Webb, June 13, 1927, copy in Hamer family papers.
6. Sterling, op. cit., 489–495.
7. Walter P. Webb to Frank Hamer, August 12, 1927, copy in Hamer family papers.
8. Webb, *Rangers*, op. cit., 545.

Chapter 16

1. Typescript, Hamer family papers.
2. Austin *Statesman*, September 24, 1929.
3. *The State Trooper*, September, 1929, 15.
4. Borger *Daily Herald*, September 13, 1929.
5. Ibid, September 18, 1929.
6. Ibid.
7. Austin *Statesman*, September 21, 1929.
8. Borger *Daily Herald*, September 23, 1929.
9. Ibid.
10. Ibid, September 29, 1929.
11. Ibid, September 30, 1930.
12. Amarillo *Globe*, September 30, 1929–
13. San Bernardino, California, *Daily Sun*, October 13, 1929.
14. Ibid.
15. Clipping, Hamer family papers.
16. Ibid.
17. Amarillo *Globe*, October 5, 1929.
18. Frank SoRelle, interview with H. Gordon Frost, El Paso, July 16, 1967.
19. Ibid; clipping, Hamer family scrapbooks.
20. Austin *Statesman*, December 2, 1929.
21. Austin *American*, clipping in Hamer family papers.

Chapter 17

1. Webb, *Rangers*, op. cit., 533, 537.
2. Ibid.
3. Frank A. Hamer, Jr., interview, op. cit.; clippings, Hamer family papers.
4. Webb, *Rangers*, op. cit., 534.
5. Original in Walter P. Webb Papers, University of Texas Archives.

6. Hamer family papers.

7. Webb, *Rangers,* op. cit., 536.

8. Ibid., 534.

9. Clipping, Hamer family scrapbook.

10. Walter P. Webb Papers, University of Texas Archives.

Chapter 18

1. *The State Trooper,* April, 1927, 11–12.

2. Ibid.

3. Clipping, Hamer family papers.

4. Frank Hamer to Gov. Dan Moody, official report, as quoted in Austin *American,* May 15, 1930.

5. Peyton, *For God and Texas,* 134–135.

6. Ibid, 135.

7. Ibid.

8. Clipping, Hamer family papers.

Chapter 19

1. Copies of letters in Hamer family papers, all dated March 30, 1931.

2. Clipping, Hamer family scrapbooks.

3. Ibid.

4. "Alaha" to Capt. Frank Hamer, 1931, original in Hamer family papers.

5. Raymond Brown, interview with H. Gordon Frost, Austin, July 12, 1967.

6. E. G. Kingsbery, interview with H. Gordon Frost, Austin, June 13, 1967.

7. Frank A. Hamer, Jr., interview, op. cit.

8. E. G. Kingsbery interview, op. cit.

9. Sterling, op. cit., 211–213.

10. Originals and copies in Hamer family papers.

11. Sen. Tom Connally to Capt. Frank Hamer, December 2, 1932, original in Hamer family papers.

12. Dan Moody statement, Hamer family papers.

13. Hon. Clem Calhoun to Sen. Morris Shepherd, December 7, 1932, carbon in Hamer family papers.

Chapter 20

1. Simmons, *Assignment Huntsville,* 129–130; Dallas *Herald,* May 23, 1934.

2. Kinney, op. cit., 88.

3. Ibid, 87–88.

4. Ibid, 87–88.

5. Ibid, 88.

6. Ibid.

7. Dallas *Herald*, May 23, 1934; Los Angeles *Evening Herald*, May 23, 1934; Houston *Post*, May 24, 1934; Kinney, op. cit., 88–89.

8. Webb and Carroll, *The Handbook of Texas*, op. cit., I, 115.

9. Ibid, II, 335.

10. Fortune, *Fugitives*, 57–61.

11. Ibid, 74–78.

12. Kinney, op. cit., 88.

13. Clipping, Hamer family papers.

14. Fortune, op. cit., 89–90.

15. Ibid, 97–103.

16. Dallas *Herald*, May 23, 1934.

17. Fortune, op. cit., 109–

18. Ibid, 111.

19. Kansas City *Star*, May 23, 1934; Dallas *Herald*, May 23, 1934; Fortune, op. cit., 110–111, 113–116.

20. Fortune, op. cit., 111–112.

21. Ibid, 122.

22. Ibid, 126.

23 Ibid, 127.

24. Kinney, op. cit., 88; Dallas *Herald*, May 23, 1934; Kansas City *Star*, May 23, 1934; Los Angeles *Evening Herald*, May 23, 1934.

25. Fortune, op. cit., 133-34; Kansas City *Star*, May 23, 1934.

26. Dallas *Herald*, May 23, 1934; Fortune, op. cit., 137–139.

27. Fortune, op. cit., 146–149.

28. Dallas *Herald*, May 23, 1934.

29. Clipping, Hamer family papers; other details in Fortune, op. cit., 149–153.

30. Fortune, op. cit., 235.

31. Simmons, op. cit., 122.

32. Houston *Post*, May 24, 1934; Dallas *Herald*, May 23, 1934.

33. Simmons, op. cit., 122.

34. Original escape notice, Huntsville, January 16, 1934, in Hamer family papers.

35. Fortune, op. cit., 221–225; Simmons, op. cit., 114–126.

36. Simmons, op. cit., 214–228.

Chapter 21

1. Gladys Hamer interview, op. cit.

2. Webb, *Rangers*, op. cit., 539–541.

3. Fortune, op. cit., 225–226.
4. Photographic reproduction, Hamer family papers.
5. Clipping, Hamer family papers.
6. Fortune, op. cit., 228.
7. Ibid.
8. Simmons, op. cit., 129–130.
9. Webb, *Rangers*, op. cit., 539.
10. Dallas *Herald*, May 23, 1934; Fortune, op. cit., 233–235.
11. Fortune, op. cit., 233–235.
12. Webb, *Rangers*, op. cit., 541-43.
13. Frank A. Hamer, Jr., interview, op. cit.
14. Webb, *Rangers*, op. cit., 543.
15. Clipping, Hamer family scrapbooks.
16. Frank A. Hamer, Jr., interview, op. cit.
17. Kansas City *Star*, May 23, 1934.
18. Austin *Daily Dispatch*, May 24, 1934.
19. Webb, *Rangers*, op. cit., 543.
20. Frank A. Hamer, Jr., interview, op. cit.

Chapter 22

1. Dallas *Journal*, May 25, 1934.
2. Clipping, Hamer family papers.
3. Simmons, op. cit., 134.
4. Ibid.
5. Frank A. Hamer, Jr., interview, op. cit.
6. San Antonio *Express*, May 24, 1934.
7. Ibid.
8. Austin *Daily Dispatch*, May 24, 1934.
9. Ibid.
10. Ibid.
11. Dallas Herald, May 24, 1934.
12. Ft. Worth *Telegram*, May 24, 1934.
13. Simmons, op. cit., 135.

Chapter 23

1. Resolution, copy in Hamer family papers.
2. Byron Utccht, "Frank Hamer, Crusader," *Texas Parade*, November, 1957, 53.
3. Austin *Statesman*, May 24, 1934.
4. Poem by J. F. Vannoy, copy in Hamer family papers.

5. Clipping, Hamer family papers.

6. Simmons, op. cit., 176–177.

7. D. S. Barker to Frank Hamer, May 26, 1934, Hamer family papers.

8. Telegram, Hamer family papers.

9. Brownwood *Bulletin*, May 26, 1934; San Antonio *Express*, May 26, 1934.

10. Texarkana *Press*, May 25, 1934.

11. Austin *Statesman*, May 25, 1934.

12. Ibid, May 26, 1934.

13. Simmons, op. cit., 163.

14. Clipping, Hamer family papers.

15. Ibid.

16. Mrs. C. H. Barrow to Capt. Frank Hamer, July 28, 1934, Hamer family papers.

17. Mrs. E. Parker to Capt. Frank Hamer, October 16, 1934, Hamer family papers.

18. Gladys Hamer interview, op. cit.; Frank A. Hamer, Jr., interview, op. cit.

19. Simmons, op. cit., 176.

20. Ibid.

21. Gladys Hamer interview, op. cit.

22. Frank A. Hamer, Jr., interview, op. cit.

23. Col. Lee Simmons and Capt. Frank Hamer to Gov. Miriam Ferguson, August 11, 1934, Hamer family papers.

24. Ibid., 114.

25. Henry Methvin to Capt. Frank Hamer, August 22, 1934, Hamer family papers.

Chapter 24

1. Roy T. Rogers interview, op. cit.

2. Ibid.

3. J. Russell Wait to Frank Hamer, January 11, 1936, Hamer family papers.

5. Frank A. Hamer, Jr., interview, op. cit.

6. Clipping, Hamer family scrapbooks.

Chapter 25

1. Telegram, September 5, 1939, in possession of Roy T. Rogers.

2. Roy T. Rogers interview, op. cit.

3. Billy Hamer to Gladys Hamer, December, 1944, Hamer family papers.

4. Gladys Hamer interview, op. cit.

5. Roy T. Rogers interview, op. cit.

6. McKay and Faulk, *Texas After Spindletop*, 200–202; The Texas *Argus*, San Antonio, Spring, 1964; Frank A. Hamer, Jr., interview, op. cit.; Gladys Hamer interview, op. cit.

7. Houston *Press*, July 12, 1955.

8. Houston *Chronicle*, July 15, 1955.
9. Roy T. Rogers interview, op. cit.
10. Dobie, "Texas Jacks," 15–16.
11. P. B. Hill, funeral eulogy, copy in Hamer family papers.
12. Webb, *Rangers*, op. cit., 519–521.
13. Ibid.
14. Dallas *News*, July 12, 1955.
15. Dan Moody statement, Hamer family papers.
16. Harold Preece, "Last of the Texas Rangers," *Guns Magazine*, December, 1955, 58.

ACKNOWLEDGMENTS

The idea for this biography originated in December 1964, when Raymond Brown, John H. Jenkins, and Mrs. Frank Hamer first met in her home in Riverside Drive in Austin. Research began early the next year when it was decided that H. Gordon Frost and John H. Jenkins would write the book and Pemberton Press would publish it. During the ensuing three years of research, many people assisted in the project. We wish particularly to express our appreciation to Mrs. Frank Hamer, Frank A. Hamer, Jr., Bill Kuykendall, Marshall Kuykendall, Roy T. Rogers, R. D. "Boss" Thorp, Harrison Hamer, Raymond Brown, E. G. Kingsbery, Bob Snow, George Allen, Frank SoRelle, and Mr. and Mrs. O. C. Dowe for granting us detailed interviews. We also wish to thank Frank Hamer III, Col. Homer Garrison, Mrs. Nell Sergent, Lan Burns, Mrs. Mary Jo Peterson, Eddie Agan, Richard Dietz, Paul Sergent, Tif Frost, Mr. and Mrs. J. Holmes Jenkins, John Pruitt, J. P. Bryan, Sr., R. B. Laws, Bob Laws, Miss Martha Chudij, Al Lowman, and—particularly—our wives, Virginia Frost and Maureen Jenkins.

BIBLIOGRAPHY

MANUSCRIPTS

Hamer Family Papers.

Walter P. Webb Papers, University of Texas Archives.

Adjutant General Papers, Texas State Archives

Ranger Records, Texas Ranger Archives.

BOOKS

Dobie, J. Frank. *Guide to Life and Literature of the Southwest.* Dallas: Southern Methodist University Press, 1952.

Fortune, Jan. *The Fugitives: The Story of Clyde Barrow and Bonnie Parker, as told by the Mother of Bonnie and the Sister of Clyde.* Dallas: Ranger Press, 1934.

Gard, Wayne. *Frontier Justice.* Norman: University of Oklahoma Press, 1949.

Hunter, J. Marvin, and N. H. Rose. *The Album of Gunfighters.* N.p., 1951.

Lea, Tom. *The King Ranch.* Boston: Little, Brown, and Company, 1957.

McKay, Seth, and Odie Faulk. *Texas After Spindletop.* Austin: Steck Company, 1965.

Neff, Pat M. *The Battles of Peace.* Ft. Worth: Pioneer Publishing Company, 1925.

Peyton, Green. *For God and Texas: The Life of P. B. Hill.* New York: McGraw Hill Book Company, 1947.

Simmons, Lee. *Assignment Huntsville: Memoirs of a Texas Prison Official.* Austin: University of Texas Press, 1957.

Sterling, W. W. *Trails and Trials of a Texas Ranger.* Austin: Privately Printed, 1959.

Webb, Walter P. *The Texas Rangers: a Century of Frontier Defence.* Boston: Houghton Mifflin Company, 1935.

Webb, Walter P., and H. Bailey Carroll (eds.). *The Handbook of Texas.* Austin: Texas State Historical Association, 1952.

White, Owen P. *Them Was the Days: From El Paso to Prohibition.* New York: Minton, Balch & Company, 1925.

PERIODICALS

Albert, Marvin H. "Killer in Skirts." *Argosy Magazine,* March 1956, 20–82.

Dobie, J. Frank. "Texas Jacks." *Texas Parade,* February, 1954, 15–16.

Griffith, Bert. "Texas Ranger." *Today Magazine,* December 15, 1934, 5–22.

Jennings, O. H. "Texas Rangers Praised: Make Short Work of Cleaning Up Oil Boom Town, Borger." *The State Trooper,* September, 1927, 15–17.

Kinney, Harrison. "Frank Hamer, Texas Ranger." *The American Gun,* 1961 (12), 82–89.

Preece, Harold. "Last of the Texas Rangers." *Guns Magazine,* December, 1955, 38–58.

Shoemaker, Kyle W. "How Mexia Was Made a Clean City." *Owenwood Magazine,* May, 1922, 19–26.

Stilwell, Hart. "Farewell Peacemaker." *True West,* Winter, 1953, 14–16.

Utrecht, Byron C. "Frank Hamer, Crusader." *Texas Parade,* November, 1957, 50–53.

NEWSPAPERS

Amarillo *Globe*

Austin *American*

Austin, *Daily Dispatch*

Borger, *Daily Herald*

Brownwood *Bulletin*

Dallas *Herald*

Dallas *News*

Del Rio *Times*

El Paso *Times*

Ft. Worth *Telegraph*

Houston *Chronicle*

Houston *Post*

Houston *Press*

Kansas City *Star*

Los Angeles *Evening Herald*

Navasota *Examiner-Review*

New York *Times*

Portland *Oregonian*

San Bernardino, California, *Daily Sun*

San Antonio *Express*

San Antonio *Texas Argus*

Texarkana *Press*

INTERVIEWS

George Allen, Lockhart, April, 1967

Raymond Brown, Austin, November, 1966

O. C. Dowe, El Paso, 1967

Frank A. Hamer, Jr., Austin, June 13, 1967

Gladys Hamer, Austin, April 14, 1967

Harrison Hamer, Giddings, July 25, 1967

Bill Kuykendall, Kyle, July 12, 1967

Marshall Kuykendall, Kyle, July 12, 1967

E. G. Kingsbery, Austin, June 13, 1967

Roy T. Rogers, Houston, June 10, 1967

Bob Snow, Ingram, June 14, 1967

Frank SoRelle, Sherman, New Mexico, 1967

R. D. "Boss" Thorp, Austin, June 13, 1967

INDEX

CPSIA information can be obtained at www.ICGtesting.com
Printed in the USA
LVOW11s0021270216

476914LV00002B/9/P